"Tami and Celine have emerged as two of my favorite cookbook authors. With *Vegan Finger Foods*, they have created something truly special. Not only are the recipes absolutely delicious, they are super fun to make! If you are looking for tasty bites to wow your guests, this will surely become your go-to book—fun, delectable, and inspiring."

—Jason Wyrick, vegan chef

"*Vegan Finger Foods* is a treasury of imaginative recipes for entertaining or for those who just want to get their hands on daring and delicious foods in bite-size morsels. Creative recipes, gorgeous photography, and a flair for the unique make this book a gem."

—Zel Allen, author of *Vegan for the Holidays*

VEGAN
FINGER FOODS

MORE THAN 100 CROWD-PLEASING RECIPES FOR BITE-SIZE EATS EVERYONE WILL LOVE

CELINE STEEN AND TAMASIN NOYES

Fair Winds Press
100 Cummings Center, Suite 406L
Beverly, MA 01915

fairwindspress.com • quarryspoon.com

First published in the USA in 2014 by
Fair Winds Press, a member of
Quarto Publishing Group USA Inc.
100 Cummings Center
Suite 406-L
Beverly, MA 01915-6101
www.fairwindspress.com

18 17 16 15 14   2 3 4 5

ISBN: 978-1-59233-594-7

Digital edition published in 2014
eISBN: 978-1-62788-014-5

Library of Congress Cataloging-in-Publication Data available

Cover and Book design by Robert Lesser
Page layout by Sporto
Photography by Celine Steen

Printed and bound in China

To all who are on the vegan journey,

whether you are taking the first step or

are well along the path

CONTENTS

CHAPTER

Mind Your Manners: Eat with Your Hands

A little preliminary info to get this finger food party started ...

• The mere idea of finger foods tends to put a smile on everyone's face: That's because most of us have happy memories of family celebrations or entertaining evenings with friends, where we were eager to dive into the tempting array of finger foods. Granted, for the majority of people that history may not have always been vegan, but this book is here to help change that!

The Irresistible Appeal of Finger Foods

We've developed fun and cruelty-free recipes that will fly in the face of "social etiquette," by making it perfectly acceptable (and quite enjoyable!) to *use our hands* as the preferred form of cutlery.

Part of the extraordinary and everlasting appeal of finger foods is that one gets to fill his or her plate to the brim with small bites and experience a wide array of exciting flavors all in one single meal. Grazing satisfies our senses and especially our taste buds: Think of it as a mini buffet, as well as a delicious vacation from boring, one-note lunches or dinners.

Mom might have wagged her finger at us and said not to play with our food, but we believe that it's actually perfectly okay to do so, even as grown-ups.

A Few Good Tips

We want to make your finger food experience an absolute blast: from planning the menu, to preparing the recipes, to finally indulging in the delicious results—the works. Nobody wants to be stuck in the kitchen while the guests are partying away in the other room with incredible food, so we've used recipe icons to show which recipes can (or should) be made in advance, whether it's just a few steps that will save you some time or entire dishes that can be prepared beforehand.

That's why we also suggest that when you prepare recipes that are a little more time-consuming, you make it easier on yourself by serving them alongside simple and healthy favorites, such as crunchy raw veggies (radishes, broccoli florets, thin asparagus spears, jicama sticks, carrot sticks, and anything else you like), as well as homemade chips and dips.

THE ORIGIN OF FINGER FOODS

Finger foods first became popular in the United States during the Prohibition era in the 1920s. Individuals who still wanted to partake in alcohol despite the amendment banning them from doing so started meeting in illegal establishments to get their boozy fix. In order to help soak up the drinks, foods that were small enough to fit in the palm of the hand were served, allowing everyone to mingle with a drink in one hand and food in the other. Although the Prohibition era ended in 1933, the popularity of finger foods lives on!

Be sure to check out our Menu Suggestions on page 164. We've matched up some recipes to suit a variety of themes to help you get started. We know that finger food is reason enough for a party in itself, but we want to make it even easier for you to get these recipes on your party table, and in your hands. Literally.

Glossary

Here is a list of a few potentially less-common ingredients you will come across in some of our recipes. Most have become easier to find in recent years, so a well-stocked grocery store should carry them. But if this isn't the case where you live, look online for sometimes better deals that, with some luck, offer free shipping as well.

Berbere: Berbere is an Ethiopian spice blend with complex flavors. It is available in well-stocked cooking stores or online. There are also many recipes available online if you prefer to make your own "house blend."

Brown rice syrup: This syrup is half as sweet as regular sugar. We especially love to use it in applications where a caramel-like flavor is desired.

Coconut milk: We use the full-fat, canned kind of coconut milk to make whipped cream by letting the cans settle at room temperature so that the cream can separate from the watery liquid, before placing them in the refrigerator for at least 24 hours. Cans of coconut milk contain anywhere between ¼ cup (60 ml) and 1 cup (235 ml) of liquid after the cream has hardened, depending on the brand. Don't throw that liquid away: it can be used in soups, to cook rice, or even to replace some or all of the water in yeast breads to make for super buttery loaves.

Coconut sugar: This minimally processed sugar can be replaced with Sucanat. Note that the switch to Sucanat will yield a slightly sweeter result.

Dry yeast: We've used both active dry yeast and instant yeast in our bread recipes. The advantage of instant yeast is that it doesn't need to be proofed before use, and can simply be added to the dry ingredients during preparation.

If you want to use instant yeast rather than active dry yeast, decrease the total amount by 25 percent. If you want to use active dry yeast rather than instant yeast, increase the total amount by 25 percent. To proof active dry yeast, combine it with the lukewarm liquids and sweetener the recipe calls for. Let stand for 5 minutes until the mixture gets bubbly, which is a sign that your yeast is good to go.

Note that we do not recommend using active dry yeast in our Green Monster Bread, Revisited (page 106).

Evaporated cane juice: We use the organic and fair trade Wholesome Sweeteners brand of evaporated cane juice, which is the chemical-, pesticide-, and cruelty-free alternative to granulated white sugar. If you know the regular white sugar in your pantry isn't processed with bone char, you can use it instead of evaporated cane juice in our recipes.

Harissa: This boldly flavored red pepper paste adds heat and depth to savory recipes. Look for it in the ethnic aisle of the grocery store and be aware that different brands have different levels of heat, so season to taste.

Korean red pepper paste: Korean red pepper paste is also known as *gochujang*, and is made from rice powder, fermented soybeans, and red peppers. This spicy paste is commonly available in the ethnic aisle of grocery stores. It can also be purchased online. Korean red pepper powder (mixed with vegetable broth) may be substituted. Start by combining ½ teaspoon powder with 1 tablespoon (15 ml) vegetable broth, then adjust to the desired heat level by adding more of either ingredient.

Mayonnaise: If the reduced-fat version of Vegenaise is available where you live, we highly recommend it because it's just as tasty as its full-fat counterpart. You can also use any favorite vegan mayonnaise, or make a good stand-in as noted in the Recipe Notes on page 91.

Neutral-flavored oils: Neutral-flavored oils are perfect in all applications, because they don't overwhelm the other flavors. Take your pick from corn oil, grapeseed oil, light olive oil, peanut oil, safflower oil, and more. Choose organic whenever available and affordable.

Nutritional yeast: Nutritional yeast comes in various sizes of flakes, which makes its weight vary depending on the brand and whether it's bought in bulk. Note that we do get ours in bulk, and the flakes are quite small, almost powderlike. If you can only find large flakes, try pulsing them a few times in a food processor before measuring, to get the best results.

Soft sun-dried tomatoes: You'll see that we use soft sun-dried tomatoes that aren't packed in oil in our recipes, mostly because we find them to be even more flavor-packed and less messy to handle than their jarred counterparts. If you can only find oil-packed sun-dried tomatoes, they're fine to use, too: Simply rinse them well, gently pat them dry, and you're good to go.

Sucanat: Sucanat is actually a brand name (standing for Sugar Cane Natural). This granular and flavorful sugar contains all of the sugarcane's molasses. We don't recommend replacing Sucanat with regular brown sugar, because the results can vary.

Tamari: Whenever possible, look for the reduced-sodium version of tamari, to have better control over the sodium levels of your food. If you cannot find tamari, use reduced-sodium soy sauce in its place.

Ume plum vinegar: Ume plum vinegar is made from the brine used from the process of pickling umeboshi plums. It's a pungent and salty liquid that brightens the flavor of a lot of dishes.

Vegan milks: Unsweetened plain almond milk is our go-to for use in any recipe that calls for vegan milk, but your own favorite vegan milk will work well, too—just be sure to use unsweetened plain for savory applications and (unsweetened or not) plain or vanilla-flavored in sweet applications.

Vegan yogurt: Depending on where you're located, it can be a struggle to find vegan yogurt at the store. You can simply replace it with the same quantity of thoroughly blended soft or firm silken tofu.

Whole wheat pastry flour: We love using whole wheat pastry flour in baked goods because it brings a little extra fiber and nutrition to the food we eat, but you can replace it at a 1:1 ratio with all-purpose flour if you prefer.

WEIGHING VERSUS MEASURING

We love to put our kitchen scales to good use to weigh most ingredients: Not only does that mean having to clean a few less measuring cups, but it also makes for far more reliable results, especially when using flour.

Recipe Icons

As you turn the pages of this book, you will come across recipes labeled as follows:

 MAKE
AHEAD

▶ ***Make Ahead:** Recipes or large components from recipes that can withstand or actually benefit from being prepared ahead of time.

 QUICK
& EASY

▶ ***Quick and Easy:** Recipes that take less than 30 minutes to whip up, provided you have intermediate cooking and/or baking skills.

 GLUTEN-FREE
POTENTIAL

▶ ***Gluten-Free Potential:** Recipes that can be free of gluten, provided the ingredients that may contain gluten are double-checked for safe use, and that the gluten-free ingredients that could have been cross-contaminated during manufacturing are purchased as certified gluten-free. We value your health and well-being, so please be extra vigilant by thoroughly checking labels and contacting companies if necessary to make sure the ingredients in question are safe to use as gluten-free.

CHAPTER

2

Veggie-Centric Finger Feasts

It's a breeze to turn virtually any vegetable into a guilt-free vegan finger food hero.

Behold, a chapter where vegetables are the main stars of this finger food show!
Seasoned to perfection, stuffed with delectable fillings, these recipes won't have
you working hard to get your five servings of vegetables a day ... or *meal*.

MAKE AHEAD QUICK & EASY  GLUTEN-FREE POTENTIAL

 QUICK & EASY  GLUTEN-FREE POTENTIAL

RASTA SALSA

Jicama is a root vegetable that we love to eat raw for its crisp texture. Here, we combine it with juicy tomatoes, creamy avocado, and all the right seasonings to create a quintessential dip that boasts the colors of the Jamaican Rastafarians. Pass the corn chips! We like to serve this salsa with our Baked Jalapeños (page 36), too.

Yield: 3½ to 4 cups (525 to 600 g) salsa

2 cups (360 g) diced, seeded tomatoes

½ cup (60 g) peeled, diced jicama

¼ cup (40 g) minced onion

2 tablespoons (30 ml) fresh lime juice

1 tablespoon (1 g) minced cilantro, or more to taste

2 or 3 cloves garlic, minced

Salt and pepper, to taste

1 avocado, halved, pitted, peeled, and diced

Combine the tomatoes, jicama, onion, lime juice, cilantro, and garlic in a medium-size bowl. Stir together. Let sit for a minimum of 1 hour at room temperature or up to 4 hours for the flavors to blend. Taste and season with salt and pepper. Gently stir in the avocado when serving.

RECIPE NOTES

- Dice the tomatoes, jicama, and avocado the same size for the best balance in flavor.

- Spice fan? Add minced jalapeño pepper to taste.

QUICKIE MARINARA

Extra easy, famously fast, and very versatile, this is a go-to in our homes to use as a pizza sauce, for dipping sandwiches or calzones, and served alongside our Twisted Bread Sticks (page 108) and Spinach Swirls (page 111). Nobody will believe you can make a sauce this flavorful in only 15 minutes. Because canned tomato sauces vary in consistency, add a tablespoon or two (17 to 33 g) of tomato paste to thicken the sauce if needed.

Yield: 1¾ cups (415 ml)

1 teaspoon olive oil

½ cup (80 g) minced onion

3 cloves garlic, minced

1 teaspoon Italian herb blend

¼ teaspoon ground black pepper

Pinch red pepper flakes

1 can (15 ounces, or 425 g) tomato sauce

Fine sea salt, to taste

Heat the oil and onion in a medium-size saucepan over medium heat. Cook until fragrant, stirring occasionally, about 3 minutes. Add the garlic, herb blend, pepper, and red pepper flakes. Cook, stirring for 2 to 3 minutes, until the garlic is fragrant, but do not brown it.

Add the sauce and reduce the heat to a simmer. Cook the sauce for 10 minutes, stirring occasionally. Taste and adjust the seasonings. The sauce may be made ahead and refrigerated in an airtight container for up to 2 days. Gently reheat over low heat if refrigerated.

BREWPUB CAULIFLOWER DIP AND CHIPS

We like to serve this dip with our own homemade pita chips, but it's also great with corn chips or vegetables for dipping. Serve with a cold beer!

Yield: 4 to 6 servings

For the chips:

2 tablespoons (30 ml) olive oil

1 tablespoon (15 ml) hot sauce (such as Frank's)

½ teaspoon smoked paprika

¼ teaspoon onion powder

Two 10-inch (25 cm) pita breads, cut into eighths

Salt, to taste (optional)

For the dip:

1 cup (235 ml) water

½ cup (70 g) raw cashews

1 tablespoon (15 ml) olive oil

½ cup (80 g) finely minced onion

¼ cup (60 g) finely minced celery

1 teaspoon smoked paprika, plus a pinch for garnish

1 teaspoon poultry seasoning

½ teaspoon dried mustard

2 tablespoons (30 ml) hot sauce (such as Frank's), or more to taste

1 cup (100 g) tiny cauliflower pieces, torn from the florets

¼ cup (20 g) old-fashioned oats

2 tablespoons (15 g) nutritional yeast

1 tablespoon (15 ml) ume plum vinegar

¼ cup (60 g) drained sauerkraut, finely chopped

1 tablespoon (10 g) minced scallion

To make the chips: Preheat the oven to 400°F (200°C, or gas mark 6). Stir together the oil, hot sauce, paprika, and onion powder in a medium-size bowl. Add the pita pieces and toss to coat. Spread on a large baking sheet in a single layer. Sprinkle with salt if desired. Bake for 10 to 12 minutes, or until nicely browned and crisp. The chips may be made ahead of time and stored in an airtight container at room temperature once completely cooled, for up to 2 days.

To make the dip: In a pot, bring the water and the cashews to a boil over high heat. Once boiling, turn off the heat and let soak for 30 minutes.

Preheat the oven to 350°F (180°C, or gas mark 4) to bake the dip. Heat the oil in a large skillet over medium heat. Cook the onion, celery, smoked paprika, poultry seasoning, and dried mustard for 2 minutes. Stir in the hot sauce and the cauliflower and turn off the heat.

Pour the cashews (with water) into a blender. Add the oats, nutritional yeast, and vinegar. Blend until completely smooth. Pour into the skillet with the vegetables and stir to combine. Stir in the sauerkraut. Pour into an 8-inch (20 cm) shallow casserole dish.

The dip may be made ahead up to this point, covered, and refrigerated for up to 24 hours. Sprinkle with the remaining pinch of smoked paprika. Bake for 30 minutes; the top will darken and may crack a little. Sprinkle with the scallions to serve.

YEAR-ROUND RATATOUILLE

We think of this as a winter ratatouille because it works well with canned tomatoes and dried herbs. However, if it's the height of summer, use peeled, seeded, diced fresh tomatoes, and adjust for the fresh herbs as indicated. We chop the vegetables small so that they are less likely to topple when eating. Serve this with slices of the Green Monster Bread, Revisited (page 106) or your favorite bread.

Yield: 2 cups (400 g)

1 tablespoon (15 ml) olive oil

¾ cup (120 g) minced onion

½ cup (41 g) finely chopped eggplant

½ cup (62 g) finely chopped zucchini

½ cup (75 g) finely chopped bell pepper (any color)

3 cloves garlic, minced

¾ teaspoon dried basil (or 2 teaspoons minced, fresh), or to taste

¾ teaspoon dried thyme (or 2 teaspoons minced, fresh), or to taste

½ teaspoon dried parsley (or 1 teaspoon minced, fresh), or to taste

½ teaspoon fine sea salt

¼ teaspoon dried rosemary (or ½ teaspoon minced, fresh), or to taste

¼ teaspoon celery seed

¼ teaspoon ground black pepper

Pinch red pepper flakes

2 tablespoons (30 ml) vegan dry red wine (optional)

1 can (14½ ounces, or 411 g) petite diced tomatoes, drained, or 1 cup (180 g) peeled, seeded, diced tomatoes

2 teaspoons minced, fresh parsley

Heat the olive oil, onion, eggplant, zucchini, bell pepper, garlic, basil, thyme, parsley, salt, rosemary, celery seed, black pepper, and red pepper flakes in a large skillet over medium heat. Cook, stirring often, for 3 to 4 minutes, until the onion is translucent. Add the red wine and cook until it is absorbed, about 3 minutes. Add the tomatoes and reduce the heat to a simmer. Cook, stirring occasionally, for 10 minutes. Stir in the 2 teaspoons fresh parsley. This is best at room temperature but benefits from sitting for 1 hour, or covered and refrigerated overnight to allow the flavors to blend.

Bring the ratatouille to room temperature for serving. Taste and adjust the seasonings when serving.

PARTY OLIVES

These are *the* olives: The ones your friends will request whenever you have a get-together. Baking the olives infuses them with incredible flavor, the almonds bring crunch, and the onions are a favorite with people who aren't even onion fans! They are easy, so flavorful, and the perfect munchable. For an even easier preparation, have the dish ready to go hours before serving. Just pop it in the oven when your guests are arriving.

Yield: 1½ cups (215 g)

½ cup (80 g) pitted green olives, pimento- or garlic-stuffed

½ cup (80 g) pitted kalamata olives

4 cipollini onions, peeled, or shallots, peeled, cut in half vertically

2 tablespoons (15 g) whole raw almonds

2 tablespoons (30 ml) vegan dry red wine or vegetable broth

4 cloves garlic

¼ to ½ teaspoon berbere, to taste

1 dundicut dried pepper or other dried pepper of choice

Preheat the oven to 400°F (200°C, or gas mark 6).

Combine all of the ingredients in a small cast-iron (or oven-proof) skillet. Bake for 25 to 30 minutes. Most of the liquid will evaporate, but don't overcook or the almonds and garlic will burn. Remove the dried pepper before serving hot or at room temperature.

RECIPE NOTES

- We like the dundicut dried peppers from Pakistan in these, but really any small dried hot pepper will do. Or substitute ¼ to ½ teaspoon red pepper flakes, to taste.

- With such simple ingredients, it's important to use the very best quality olives that you can afford.

RAINBOW ROOT VEGGIE CHIPS

We love the colorful batches of deliciously crispy chips this recipe yields! You can use whichever root vegetable you love the most here. Note that they are best enjoyed fresh, as soon as they're cool enough to eat. So invite a few friends over if you're in the mood for sharing, or bring your own appetite to the table, and munch away. All the flavored salts here also work like a charm in most of our recipes, as long as the flavors pair well. We've indicated where they're an especially perfect match, so don't be afraid of the larger batches they yield. If the recipes really do make too much for your taste, it's a breeze to halve or even quarter them.

Yield: 6 to 8 servings, ½ cup (146 g) of each flavored salt

For the citrus thyme salt:

½ cup (146 g) fine sea salt

Zest from 2 medium-size organic lemons

Fresh thyme leaves from approximately 20 sprigs

1 teaspoon garlic powder

1½ teaspoons granulated onion

For the smoked paprika salt:

½ cup (146 g) fine sea salt

1½ teaspoons smoked paprika

For the rosemary orange salt:

½ cup (146 g) fine sea salt

1 teaspoon onion powder

Zest of 1 organic orange

Fresh rosemary leaves from 2 twigs

To make any flavor of the salts: Combine the ingredients listed under the flavor in a food processor, and pulse several times. Transfer into an airtight jar. It will keep indefinitely at room temperature.

To make the chips: Wash the vegetables and dry them thoroughly; this will ensure they will be crisp once fried, and will minimize oil splatters as the chips are frying. Trim a little less than 1 inch (2.5 cm) from the root ends of all veggies, a little less for the potatoes, then peel them. (Keep the trimmed bits for soup, broth, or compost!) Using a mandoline, cut the vegetables to approximately $\frac{1}{16}$ inch (1.6 mm) thickness: The thinner the veggies, the quicker the frying. Make sure that all the slices are of the same thickness. Use caution when working with the mandoline; these things are sharp!

Before frying the veggies, have a colander handy, and line it with a generous amount of paper towels.

Heat about 3 inches (7.5 cm) of oil in a deep fryer or large-size, heavy-bottomed pot over high heat to 350°F (180°C). Use a thermometer to measure the temperature, and use caution with the hot oil. Fry the veggies in small batches so that the temperature doesn't decrease too much, which would cause soggy chips. Stick to one kind of vegetable per batch. The cooking time should be approximately 2 to 3 minutes for each kind of chip. The chips are ready when they are golden brown, the bubbling slows down, and the edges of the chips are curled.

For the chips:

1 sweet potato (approximately 1 pound, or 454 g)

2 small beets (approximately 8 ounces, or 227 g)

1 parsnip (approximately 8 ounces, or 227 g)

1 turnip (approximately 8 ounces, or 227 g)

2 purple potatoes (approximately 8 ounces, or 227 g)

Peanut oil or corn oil, for frying

Use a slotted spoon to place the chips in the paper towel–lined colander to absorb the excess oil, sprinkle with a really small pinch of either one of the salts (it's easy to go overboard with the salt, so be careful), and shake the veggies in the paper towels, holding all the corners of the towels, so that the veggies get lightly dusted with the salt, and so that they get rid of the excess oil to become as crisp as can be.

Replace the paper towels if they get saturated with excess oil. You can also use two colanders lined with paper towels, so that the salt flavors don't mix. Once the shaking is done, transfer the chips to a cooling rack that has a grid pattern with $\frac{1}{2}$-inch (1.3 cm) holes, or smaller, so that the smaller chips don't fall through the holes. Let cool, and repeat with new batches of veggies until you run out. Serve as soon as the chips are cool enough to eat.

MAKE AHEAD QUICK & EASY  GLUTEN-FREE POTENTIAL

MARINATED MUSHROOMS

It may not be the norm in most recipes for marinated mushrooms, but we absolutely love keeping the mushrooms uncooked here. Their fresh flavor is enhanced by the sprinkling of herbs, while the oil and vinegar infuse them with flavor and a crisp acidity.

Yield: 4 servings

2 tablespoons (30 ml) red wine vinegar

1 tablespoon (15 ml) olive oil

1 tablespoon (10 g) finely minced shallot

1 tablespoon (15 ml) fresh lemon juice

2 cloves garlic, minced

¼ teaspoon dried basil

¼ teaspoon dried oregano

¼ teaspoon agave nectar

¼ teaspoon fine sea salt

¼ teaspoon ground black pepper

Pinch red pepper flakes

12 ounces (340 g) button mushrooms, cut in half or quarters if large

¾ teaspoon minced fresh parsley

Combine the vinegar, oil, shallot, lemon juice, garlic, basil, oregano, agave, salt, black pepper, and red pepper flakes in a large skillet. Bring to a boil and cook for 2 minutes, stirring. Do not brown the garlic. Remove from the heat. Add the mushrooms and parsley, stirring to coat well. Transfer to an airtight container and refrigerate for 1 hour, or up to 2 days. Taste and adjust the seasonings upon serving.

MEDITERRANEAN STUFFED MUSHROOMS

Juicy, seasoned mushrooms are stuffed with bright spinach, sweet onion, complex sun-dried tomatoes, and salty olives, all in a barley base to create this luscious appetizer. Quinoa may be substituted for the barley, if desired. Cook the quinoa according to package directions.

Yield: 8 to 10 mushrooms

3 cups (705 ml) vegetable broth

¼ cup (50 g) uncooked pearl barley

Fine sea salt, to taste

1 tablespoon (9 g) pine nuts

1 tablespoon plus 1 teaspoon (20 ml) olive oil, divided

2 tablespoons (30 ml) vegan dry red wine or vegetable broth, divided

¼ teaspoon ground black pepper, plus extra to taste

8 to 10 stuffing mushrooms (each measuring 2 inches, or 5 cm)

2 cups (80 g) packed fresh spinach, chopped

⅓ cup (55 g) minced onion

3 tablespoons (12 g) soft sun-dried tomato halves (not oil-packed), minced

2 cloves garlic, minced

1 tablespoon (10 g) minced kalamata olives

1 teaspoon dried Italian herb blend

Pinch red pepper flakes

Juice from ½ fresh lemon (about 2½ teaspoons, or 12.5 ml)

Combine the broth, barley, and a pinch of salt in a medium-size saucepan over high heat. Bring to a boil, then reduce the heat to a simmer and cook, stirring occasionally, for 50 minutes, or until tender and the water is absorbed.

Preheat the oven to 375°F (190°C, or gas mark 5). Heat the pine nuts in a small skillet over medium heat. Cook and stir until golden, about 4 minutes.

Stir together 1 tablespoon (15 ml) of the olive oil, 1 tablespoon (15 ml) of the wine, and the pepper in a 9-inch (23 cm) baking dish. Remove the stems from the mushrooms (do not discard!), and add the caps to the baking dish, turning to coat. Arrange so the stemmed sides are facing up. Mince the mushroom stems.

Heat the remaining 1 teaspoon olive oil in a large skillet over medium heat. Add the mushroom stems, spinach, onion, sun-dried tomatoes, garlic, olives, herb blend, and red pepper flakes. Stir and cook until the spinach is wilted, 3 to 5 minutes. Stir in the lemon juice and barley. Add salt and pepper to taste. Fill each mushroom with about 2 teaspoons filling, mounding the filling in the mushrooms. There may be a small amount of leftover filling. It may be spooned over the mushrooms if desired. Top the mushrooms with the pine nuts, pressing them lightly into the filling. Pour the remaining 1 tablespoon (15 ml) wine into the baking dish and cover with foil. Bake for 30 minutes. Remove the foil carefully, as it will be steamy. Bake uncovered for 15 minutes longer, or until the mushrooms are tender and the pine nuts are toasted. Serve warm or at room temperature.

BLACK LENTIL ENDIVE CUPS

Fresh, crisp endive leaves are the ideal base for these elegant and well-seasoned lentils. The drizzle adds yet another layer of flavor, as well as a creaminess. For easy entertaining, both the lentil filling and the drizzle can be made up to 2 days in advance. Pull them out of the refrigerator, assemble, and you'll be sitting with your guests in minutes.

Yield: 20 lentil cups

For the lentil cups:

2 cups (470 ml) water

½ cup (96 g) dry baby beluga lentils

1 clove garlic, minced

1 tablespoon (10 g) finely minced onion

¼ teaspoon ground coriander

¼ teaspoon ground cumin

¼ teaspoon fine sea salt

⅛ teaspoon smoked paprika

Juice from ½ fresh lemon

1 tablespoon (15 ml) seasoned rice vinegar

Salt and pepper, to taste

20 fresh endive leaves, separated

For the drizzle:

¼ cup (35 g) raw cashews, soaked in water for 3 hours, drained

1½ tablespoons (23 ml) water, plus more as needed

1 teaspoon fresh lemon juice, plus more to taste

1 teaspoon seasoned rice vinegar

1 teaspoon nutritional yeast

1 teaspoon medium miso

1 teaspoon Sriracha, or more to taste

To make the lentils: Combine the water, lentils, and garlic in a small saucepan. Bring to a boil over high heat. Reduce to a simmer and cook for 18 minutes, or until the lentils are tender but still hold their shape. Drain. Transfer the lentils to a medium-size bowl and add the onion, spices, lemon juice, and rice vinegar. Stir to combine, and refrigerate for at least 1 hour for the flavors to meld. The filling can be covered and refrigerated for up to 2 days.

To make the drizzle: Process all the ingredients together in a blender until completely smooth. Add extra water if needed to get a drizzle consistency. Taste and adjust the seasoning to suit your tastes. Transfer the mixture to a small zip-style plastic bag. Refrigerate until serving, or up to 3 days. Adjust the consistency when serving.

To assemble, taste the lentils and season with salt and pepper if needed. Spoon a generous 2 teaspoons of lentils onto the center of each leaf. Cut a small corner off the zip-style plastic bag filled with the drizzle, and squeeze the drizzle over the lentil cups as desired.

HARISSA CARROT ZUCCHINI CUPS

With Moroccan influences thanks to the harissa, a North-African chili sauce and condiment, this is a new take on zesty carrot salad. For convenience, the salad can be made ahead of time and refrigerated in a covered container for up to 24 hours. When serving, the grilled zucchini cups are topped with raisins to bring a kiss of sweetness to this lightly smoky, spiced-to-perfection starter.

Yield: 12 zucchini cups

2 zucchini (7 inches [18 cm] long, 1 to 1½ inches [2.5 to 3.7 cm] wide)

1 tablespoon (15 ml) tamari

½ teaspoon liquid smoke

½ teaspoon olive oil

½ teaspoon ground coriander

Nonstick cooking spray

2 teaspoons harissa paste, or more to taste

2 teaspoons red wine vinegar

1 cup (110 g) grated carrot

2 teaspoons fresh minced parsley

Salt and pepper, to taste

36 raisins

Cut the ends from the zucchini, then cut each into six 1-inch (2.5 cm) rounds. Using a sharp paring knife, a metal measuring spoon, or a melon baller, cut the center of each slice into a cup, leaving the edges and bottom intact.

Stir together the tamari, liquid smoke, oil, and coriander in a small bowl. Heat a grill pan over medium-high heat. Lightly coat the pan with cooking spray. Brush the cut sides of the zucchini with the tamari mixture. Put the rounds on the grill with the cup side down. Grill until marked, about 4 minutes. Turn one-quarter turn and grill again until marked, 3 to 4 minutes. Baste and turn over to grill the smooth sides of the rounds for 3 to 4 minutes until marked. Turn one-quarter turn and grill again until marked. Remove the rounds from the grill. The zucchini should retain their texture rather than be overly soft.

Stir the harissa and vinegar into the remaining basting liquid. Pour over the carrot, and add the parsley. Stir to combine, and season to taste with salt and pepper. Add more harissa, if desired.

Spoon the mixture evenly into the zucchini cups, mounding the mixture. Top each with three raisins, and serve warm.

TREE-HUGGER CELERY STICKS

A giant leap from the peanut butter-stuffed celery of our youth, this quinoa and tofu version disappears just as quickly. They are fresh and smoky all at once, and the celery is a crunchy way to get the tasty filling to your mouth. Because celery stalks come in various sizes, you may need a different number of them than called for here. These can be made ahead of time and stored in a covered container in the refrigerator for up to 12 hours before serving.

Yield: 28 to 34 pieces

½ cup (120 ml) vegetable broth

¼ cup (43 g) dry quinoa, rinsed

1 teaspoon ground cumin

½ teaspoon smoked paprika

½ teaspoon dried oregano

½ teaspoon smoked salt

2 teaspoons olive oil

¼ cup (40 g) minced onion

¼ teaspoon ground black pepper, plus extra to taste

3 ounces (85 g) extra-firm tofu, drained, mashed

Juice from ½ fresh lemon

Fine sea salt, to taste

8 to 10 stalks organic celery, trimmed

3 peppadew peppers or pickled red cherry peppers, rinsed and patted dry, chopped

Heat the broth, quinoa, cumin, paprika, oregano, and smoked salt in a small saucepan until boiling. Reduce the heat to simmer and cook, stirring occasionally, for about 15 minutes, until the tails have sprouted and the broth is absorbed. Transfer to a medium-size bowl.

Heat the oil in a small skillet over medium heat. Cook the onion and black pepper, stirring occasionally, until translucent, about 4 minutes. Add to the quinoa mixture. Stir in the mashed tofu and lemon juice, combining well. Taste and adjust the seasonings.

Cover and refrigerate for at least 1 hour (or up to 24 hours) for the flavors to meld. Pack the filling into the celery stalks and cut into 2-inch (5 cm) pieces. Sprinkle evenly with the peppadew peppers.

MINI BELL PEPPER BOATS

These little boats are the perfect summery snack: crunchy fresh veggies packed full of a flavorful creamy filling, and sprinkled with refreshing fresh parsley. Note that the filling can be made without chickpeas and used as a spread on bread: We love it on pumpernickel!

Yield: 40 bell pepper boats, 2½ cups (600 g) filling

¼ cup (40 g) pitted kalamata olives

4 large pitted, garlic-stuffed or regular green olives

1 tablespoon (4 g) soft sun-dried tomato halves (not oil-packed)

1 teaspoon capers, without brine

2 or 3 cloves garlic, pressed, to taste

1 scant teaspoon dried basil

1 can (15 ounces, or 425 g) chickpeas, drained and rinsed

Juice from ½ fresh lemon (about 2½ teaspoons, or 12.5 ml)

1 tablespoon (15 ml) tamari

½ teaspoon liquid smoke

1¼ cups (335 g) Cashew Almond Spread (page 121)

Salt and pepper, to taste

20 organic multicolored mini bell peppers, halved, trimmed, rinsed, and patted dry

⅓ cup (20 g) fresh parsley, minced

Finely chop the olives, sun-dried tomatoes, and capers. Place them in a large bowl, along with the garlic. Rub the dried basil between your fingers while adding it on top of the chopped olive mix, and stir to combine. Set aside.

Place the chickpeas, lemon juice, tamari, and liquid smoke in a medium-size skillet. Cook over medium heat, stirring occasionally, until the liquids have evaporated, about 5 minutes. This will flavor the chickpeas and also make them easier to crush.

Coarsely crush the chickpeas with a potato masher: You don't want them completely mashed, just not left whole. Add the Cashew Almond Spread and chickpeas to the olive mix. Stir to thoroughly combine, and season with salt and pepper to taste. Cover, and refrigerate for at least 2 hours or overnight to let the flavors meld and the mixture firm up.

Fill the bell pepper halves with 1 tablespoon (15 g) filling, or however much will generously fit, and sprinkle parsley on top. Serve immediately, or store in the refrigerator until ready to serve. Cover and store leftovers in the refrigerator for up to 3 days.

RECIPE NOTE

All vegetables vary in size, so you might want to play it safe and have a few extra just in case. Otherwise, the filling is also delicious on bread if you have leftovers but no veggies left to use it in.

SERVING SUGGESTIONS & VARIATIONS

If you prefer using hollowed Roma tomato halves here, it will be perfect, too. You will need approximately 8 tomatoes (about 24 ounces, or 680 g). You should be able to fit about 1½ tablespoons (23 g) of filling per tomato half.

KALE CUCUMBER CUPS

Hurray, kale! The most super of the superfoods! We love the crisp cucumber slices with the seasoned (to-your-taste) kale, but if pressed, we'll admit to eating this simply as a kale salad. For prettier presentation, score the cucumber with a fork before cutting into rounds. The kale salad can be made ahead of time and stored in a covered container in the refrigerator for up to 8 hours, but it will continue to reduce in amount, so make extra.

Yield: 14 cups

2 cups (120 g) packed very finely chopped kale leaves (stems discarded)

2 teaspoons tamari

2 teaspoons fresh lemon juice

1 teaspoon toasted sesame oil

½ teaspoon Sriracha, or more to taste

½ teaspoon white sesame seeds, more to taste

Salt and pepper, to taste

14 ½-inch (1.3 cm) thick round slices organic cucumber (see headnote)

Stir together the kale, tamari, and lemon juice in a medium-size bowl. Using your hands, rub it together for a few minutes, or until the kale wilts and softens. Stir in the sesame oil, Sriracha, and sesame seeds. Let sit for 15 minutes for the flavors to meld. The kale will reduce in amount. Using a ½-teaspoon measuring spoon or a melon baller, carefully scoop out the center of the cucumbers to create a bowl. Do not scoop all the way through the cucumber. Taste the salad and adjust the seasonings. Fill each cucumber with 1 teaspoon kale salad.

SERVING SUGGESTIONS & VARIATIONS

Serve these with Pantry Raid Ranch Dip (page 57) for even more flavor.

RECIPE NOTE

Although we prefer organic cucumbers, if they aren't available (or are too pricy), be sure to peel them instead of scoring them.

BAKED JALAPEÑOS

Creamy filling is hidden by a crunchy coating, all inside a spicy jalapeño, making an easy snack
with layers of flavor and texture. If desired, serve these with the Rasta Salsa (page 16). Safety first:
Wear plastic gloves when handling the peppers!

**Yield: 16 to 24 pepper halves,
⅔ cup (200 g) filling**

For the filling:

½ cup (70 g) raw cashews, soaked in ½ cup
(120 ml) water for 3 hours, drained

½ cup (131 g) cooked navy beans

2 tablespoons (30 ml) vegan dry white wine

2 tablespoons (30 ml) fresh lemon juice

1 tablespoon (8 g) nutritional yeast flakes

2 teaspoons ume plum vinegar

1 teaspoon light miso

½ teaspoon onion powder

Salt and pepper, to taste

For the peppers:

Nonstick cooking spray

8 to 12 medium-size whole jalapeño peppers

2 cups (56 g) organic cornflakes, crushed

½ cup (40 g) whole wheat panko crumbs

Rasta Salsa (page 16), for serving

To make the filling: Combine all the ingredients in a blender
or food processor, and process until completely smooth. Cover
and refrigerate for at least 1 hour for the flavors to meld. Taste
and adjust the seasonings. This can be made up to 4 days in
advance. Store covered in the refrigerator.

If baking right away, preheat the oven to 400°F (200°C,
or gas mark 6). If preparing in advance, the peppers may be
stuffed and coated, then refrigerated for 24 hours before
baking.

To make the peppers: Lightly coat a baking sheet with
cooking spray. Cut the peppers in half and remove the seeds.
Fill each half with up to 1 tablespoon (17 g) filling, depending
on the size of the halves. Stir together the cornflakes and the
panko on a plate.

Dip the filling-stuffed side of each pepper into the cornflake
mixture, patting the crumbs to adhere to the filling. Bake the
peppers for 20 minutes, until the crumbs are golden brown and
the peppers are slightly deflated. Serve with the salsa.

SESAME CUCUMBER SANDWICHES

The filling can be made ahead, covered, and refrigerated for up to 24 hours. The cucumbers can be sliced ahead of time, too, but it's best to fill the sandwiches near serving time so the cucumber doesn't get too soft.

Yield: 24 sandwiches

4 ounces (113 g) tempeh, crumbled

1 cup (235 ml) water

1 tablespoon (15 ml) tamari

2 teaspoons toasted sesame oil

1 teaspoon sesame chile oil

¼ to ½ teaspoon Chinese five-spice powder, to taste

½ teaspoon grated fresh ginger

1 clove garlic, minced

¼ cup (40 g) finely chopped snow peas

1 tablespoon (7 g) grated carrot

1 tablespoon (10 g) minced scallion

2 tablespoons (30 g) vegan mayonnaise

½ teaspoon Sriracha, more to taste

Salt and pepper, to taste

48 very thin round slices organic cucumber (about 2 English cucumbers)

3 tablespoons (24 g) black sesame seeds

Bring the tempeh, water, and tamari to a boil in a small skillet over high heat. Reduce the heat to medium and continue to boil until all the liquid is absorbed, about 15 minutes. Transfer the tempeh to a plate, and wipe the skillet dry with a paper towel. Add the oils to the skillet, and return to medium heat. Add the tempeh, and cook, stirring occasionally, until lightly browned, about 5 minutes. Stir in the ¼ teaspoon five-spice powder, ginger, and garlic and cook for 1 minute longer. Taste a piece of the tempeh, and add the remaining ¼ teaspoon five-spice powder if desired. Remove from the heat and let cool.

In a medium-size bowl, combine the cooled tempeh mixture, snow peas, carrot, scallion, mayonnaise, and Sriracha. Taste and adjust the seasonings. Scoop 1 teaspoon of the filling onto half of the cucumber slices. Top with the remaining cucumber slices and press down so the filling reaches the edges of the cucumber. Roll the filling part in the sesame seeds so the seeds will adhere to the middle of the sandwich. Gently press the filling back to line up with the cucumbers. Refrigerate until ready to serve, up to 1 hour.

SERVING SUGGESTIONS & VARIATIONS

Replace the tempeh with 4 ounces (113 g) cooked chickpeas. Add the chickpeas, 1 tablespoon (15 ml) tamari, 1 teaspoon toasted sesame oil, and ½ teaspoon sesame chile oil to a small skillet. Cook over medium-high heat for 2 minutes, until the liquid partially evaporates; turn down the heat to medium, add the spice, ginger, and garlic, and cook until browned, about 2 minutes. The oil might spit while cooking, so use a splatter screen. Coarsely crush the chickpeas with a fork until they resemble crumbled tempeh. Let cool. Continue with the recipe as above.

POTATO PUFFS WITH TAPENADE

This recipe is designed to use the insides of the potatoes from the Nacho Potato Skins (page 44). But if you have other potatoes in mind (or in the refrigerator), use about 2 cups (244 g) cooked potato pieces. Bonus: The tapenade is sensational on bread, too.

Yield: 14 to 18 puffs, ⅓ cup (85 g) tapenade

For the tapenade:

¼ cup (40 g) pitted kalamata olives

4 large pitted green olives

1 tablespoon (4 g) soft sun-dried tomato halves (not oil-packed)

3 leaves fresh basil

Pinch ground black pepper

For the puffs:

Nonstick cooking spray

Potato insides from Nacho Potato Skins (page 44) (about 2 cups, or 244 g)

½ cup (40 g) organic vegan instant potatoes

½ cup (120 ml) unsweetened plain vegan milk

2 tablespoons (30 ml) olive oil

½ teaspoon fine sea salt

Generous pinch ground black pepper

To make the tapenade: Finely chop all the ingredients, and stir together. A mini blender may also be used on pulse. Set aside. The tapenade can be stored in the refrigerator, covered, for up to 4 days.

To make the puffs: Preheat the oven to 400°F (200°C, or gas mark 6). Lightly coat a mini muffin pan with cooking spray. Heat the potato pieces, instant potatoes, milk, and oil in a medium-size saucepan over medium heat. Cook for 2 to 3 minutes, mashing the potatoes as they cook. The mixture should easily form a ball. Season with salt and pepper. When the mixture is cool enough to handle comfortably, scoop 1 tablespoon (47 g) into your hand and form into a small ball. Make a small indentation with your finger. Spoon ½ teaspoon tapenade into the indentation. Seal the ball closed with another 1 to 1½ teaspoons potato mixture. Roll closed and put in the mini muffin pan. Continue until all of the potato mixture is used. You will have extra tapenade for another use, such as a sandwich spread. Lightly coat the balls with cooking spray and bake for 35 minutes, or until lightly browned and slightly crusty. Serve warm or at room temperature.

NACHO POTATO SKINS

Potato skins, the epitome of bar finger food, get a cleaned-up, cruelty-free remake that doesn't miss a beat in flavor. Save the insides of the potatoes to make Potato Puffs, page 43.

Yield: 12 potato skins

6 medium-size russet potatoes (each about 5 ounces, or 140 g)

1 can (15 ounces, or 425 g) black beans, drained and rinsed

½ cup (90 g) chopped tomato

¼ cup (40 g) minced red onion

2 tablespoons (18 g) minced poblano pepper

2 tablespoons (30 ml) fresh lime juice

2 teaspoons minced fresh cilantro, or more to taste

½ teaspoon ground cumin

Salt and pepper, to taste

2 tablespoons (30 ml) olive oil

1 tablespoon (15 ml) canned chipotle pepper in adobo, with sauce

1 recipe Nacho Saucy Dip (page 58) (see Recipe Note)

1 medium avocado, pitted, peeled, and diced (optional)

Preheat the oven to 400°F (200°C, or gas mark 6). Pierce the potatoes a couple of times so they can release steam. Bake the potatoes for 45 minutes, or 1 hour if larger. The potatoes should be tender. Let cool, slice in half, and scoop the insides from the potatoes, leaving about ¼ inch (6 mm) from the skin intact. While the potatoes are cooling, prepare the filling.

Stir together the beans, tomato, onion, pepper, lime juice, cilantro, and cumin in a medium-size bowl. Season to taste with salt and pepper.

Preheat the oven to 475°F (240°C, or gas mark 9). Combine the olive oil and chipotle in a mortar and pestle, and pound until combined. Add a pinch of salt and pepper. Pierce the inside of the potato skins a few times with a fork. Brush the oil on the insides of the potatoes, and place on a baking sheet. Bake for 15 minutes, or until starting to crisp. For extra crispness, broil the potato skins for a few minutes after baking. Fill each potato with a heaping tablespoon (28 g) of filling, dividing the filling evenly among the potatoes. Top each potato with Nacho Saucy Dip and a few pieces of avocado.

RECIPE NOTE

If you plan on serving this as a gluten-free dish, be sure to double-check that all of your ingredients are certified gluten-free, and that your guests who suffer from celiac disease are okay with the oat flour used in the Nacho Saucy Dip. Many celiac sufferers can also be sensitive to oats, even when those are purchased as certified gluten-free. This sensitivity is due to the fact that oats contain a protein called avenin, which is molecularly similar to wheat protein. If there are any diners with celiac, simply serve the sauce on the side.

CORN FRITTERS WITH TOMATO-THYME GRAVY

We like to serve these with Tomato Thyme Gravy, but if you're short on time, just spike some vegan mayonnaise with hot sauce, and dip away! If you happen to have extra gravy, save it to pour over a tofu scramble, or use it as a dip with the Baked Frittata Minis (page 72).

Yield: 16 to 18 fritters, 2 cups (470 ml) gravy

For the fritters:

½ cup (60 g) garbanzo flour

¼ cup (31 g) all-purpose flour

2 tablespoons (15 g) fine cornmeal (not corn flour)

½ teaspoon baking powder

½ teaspoon ground cumin

¼ teaspoon dried thyme

¼ teaspoon paprika

¼ teaspoon fine sea salt

Generous pinch ground black pepper

1 cup (135 g) frozen corn kernels, thawed

2 tablespoons (14 g) finely grated carrot

1 tablespoon plus 1 teaspoon (4 g) minced chives, plus more for garnish, if desired

¼ cup (60 ml) unsweetened plain vegan milk, more if needed

High-heat neutral-flavored oil, for cooking

For the tomato-thyme gravy:

½ cup (80 g) finely minced onion

2 tablespoons (16 g) all-purpose flour

2 tablespoons (30 ml) olive oil

1 teaspoon dried thyme or 1 tablespoon (2 g) minced fresh thyme

½ teaspoon fine sea salt

¼ teaspoon ground black pepper

1 can (15 ounces, or 425 g) diced tomatoes with juice, preferably no salt added

¾ cup (180 ml) tomato juice

1 tablespoon (15 ml) Frank's Hot Sauce, or more, to taste

2 teaspoons liquid smoke

To make the fritters: Combine the flours, cornmeal, baking powder, spices, salt, and pepper in medium-size bowl. Whisk to combine. Stir in the corn, carrot, and chives, followed by the milk. The mixture will be sticky, but it should be shapeable. If not, add an extra 1 tablespoon (15 ml) milk.

Pour a thin layer of oil into a large skillet. Heat over medium-high heat. Using a heaping tablespoon (20 g) of the mixture, shape into a small patty about 1½ inches (4 cm) across and ½- to ¾-inch (1.3 to 2 cm) thick. Put the fritters into the oil and cook until golden, 4 to 6 minutes. Turn the fritters over to cook the second side, 4 to 6 minutes.

Drain on a paper towel and serve with the gravy.

To make the tomato-thyme gravy: Heat the onion, flour, oil, thyme, salt, and pepper in a medium-size saucepan over medium heat. Cook, stirring, for 3 to 4 minutes, until the flour is cooked. Add the remaining ingredients, and simmer over low heat for 15 to 20 minutes. The gravy may be made ahead, covered, and refrigerated for up to 48 hours. Heat over low heat to serve.

OVEN-STEAMED ARTICHOKES WITH AWESOME SAUCE

This sauce is also a terrific dipping sauce for steamed asparagus. The stem of the artichoke can be trimmed, peeled, and steamed in the broth, too.

Yield: 4 servings, ¼ cup (57 g) sauce

2 small artichokes (3 to 4 inches [7.5 to 10 cm] in diameter)

1 lemon, cut in half

6 cloves garlic

2 tablespoons (30 ml) olive oil, divided

½ teaspoon Citrus Thyme Salt (page 24) or fine sea salt

¼ teaspoon ground black pepper

½ cup (120 ml) vegetable broth, more if needed

2 sprigs fresh thyme

1 tablespoon (15 g) Dijon mustard

1 teaspoon capers, drained

½ teaspoon nutritional yeast

Preheat the oven to 425°F (220°C, or gas mark 7).

Trim the artichokes by cutting off the top 1 inch (2.5 cm) or so. Using kitchen scissors, trim the pointed ends off the leaves. Wash the artichokes under cold water, prying them open gently, but not pulling them apart. Shake the water off, and dry with a kitchen towel. Rub all cut parts immediately with the cut lemon. Poke 3 garlic cloves into each artichoke, nestling them between the leaves. Put the artichokes in a large cast-iron skillet or baking dish and drizzle each with 1 tablespoon (15 ml) olive oil. Sprinkle with salt and pepper, then put the cut side of the lemon down on top of the artichoke. Pour the broth into the skillet, add the thyme sprigs, and cover tightly with foil.

Bake for 30 minutes and check the broth level, adding an additional ⅓ cup (80 ml) if needed. Bake for 30 minutes longer, then check to see if the outer leaves are tender. If not, add more broth to the skillet, and cover again. Bake for 15 minutes longer and check again. Larger artichokes take slightly longer to cook.

When the artichokes are done, remove the garlic cloves and put them in a small blender. Add the mustard, 2 teaspoons (4 g) of baked lemon pulp, capers, and nutritional yeast. Discard the thyme from the broth. Add 3 tablespoons (45 ml) of the broth from the skillet to the mixture. Blend until smooth. Serve the sauce alongside the artichokes for dipping.

GREEN BEANS JALFREZI

Simple ingredients combine to create a fresh, small plate bursting with flavor. If you prefer your Indian food with a little heat, feel free to add ¼ to ½ teaspoon red pepper flakes with the onion.

Yield: 4 servings

1 teaspoon olive oil (not needed if your wok or pan is well seasoned)

1 pound (454 g) fresh green beans, trimmed, cut into bite-size pieces

3 tablespoons (45 ml) vegetable broth, more if needed

¼ cup (40 g) chopped red onion

1 cup (180 g) chopped and seeded tomato

2 cloves garlic, minced

1 teaspoon minced fresh ginger

½ teaspoon mild, medium, or hot curry powder

Salt and pepper, to taste

Minced fresh cilantro, for garnish (optional)

Heat the oil in a wok or cast-iron skillet over high heat. Add the beans and cook, stirring, for 3 to 5 minutes, until black spots start to appear. Add the broth, onion, tomato, garlic, ginger, and curry powder. Cook for 5 minutes, or until most of the broth has evaporated and the beans are tender but still firm. Add a little more broth if needed. Cook until the tomatoes have broken down a little, 3 to 5 minutes, stirring frequently. Season with salt and pepper, garnish with cilantro, and serve.

TAHINI CAULIFLOWER

Just a few spices are needed to make this eye-catching cauliflower dish. It would also be golden (literally, not just figuratively) as a side dish, if preferred. If you have leftovers, cover the cauliflower and store in the refrigerator for up to 2 days. Let the cauliflower come to room temperature before serving.

Yield: 4 servings

Nonstick cooking spray

¼ cup (60 ml) seasoned rice vinegar

2 tablespoons (32 g) tahini

2 teaspoons light agave nectar

1 teaspoon ground coriander

½ teaspoon turmeric

½ teaspoon fine sea salt

Generous pinch red pepper flakes

5 cups (500 g) bite-size cauliflower florets (1 medium head)

Preheat the oven to 400°F (200°C, or gas mark 6). Lightly coat a large baking sheet (or two smaller ones) with cooking spray.

Blend the vinegar, tahini, agave, coriander, turmeric, salt, and pepper flakes in a mini blender. Put the cauliflower in a large bowl, and pour the mixture over the florets. Stir well to coat. Spread the florets in a single layer on the baking sheet. Bake for 15 minutes, or to desired tenderness. Serve hot, warm, or at room temperature.

GLAZED SUGAR SNAPS

We'll confess to eating these with our fingers when we're with close friends, but will understand if you prefer a fork or chopsticks! The glaze is versatile: Try it with asparagus or green beans.

Yield: 4 servings

- 1½ tablespoons (23 ml) tamari
- 1½ tablespoons (23 ml) seasoned rice vinegar
- 1½ teaspoons pure maple syrup
- 1½ teaspoons light miso
- ¾ teaspoon Sriracha, or more to taste
- 1 teaspoon cornstarch
- 1 pound (454 g) fresh sugar snap peas, trimmed
- 3 cloves garlic, minced
- ¾ teaspoon minced fresh ginger
- ½ teaspoon toasted sesame oil
- ½ teaspoon toasted sesame seeds

Whisk together the tamari, vinegar, maple syrup, miso, Sriracha, and cornstarch in a small bowl.

In a wok or dry skillet over high heat, cook the sugar snap peas, stirring frequently, until black spots appear, about 3 minutes. Do not overcook. Add the garlic, ginger, sesame oil, and sesame seeds. Cook, stirring, for 1 minute. Add the tamari mixture. Cook and stir until thickened, about 2 minutes. Serve hot, warm, or at room temperature.

BRUSSELS SPROUTS WITH CRISPY ONIONS

A bright, creamy sauce is drizzled over crispy onions and cooked-to-perfection Brussels sprouts in this sensational small plate. Yes, this one needs a fork, but with small plates all the fashion, we wanted to include a few recipes for them here. Try not to have fork fights over the last bites.

Yield: 4 servings

- 2 tablespoons (28 g) vegan mayonnaise
- ½ teaspoon Dijon mustard
- 2 teaspoons fresh lemon juice
- Salt and pepper, to taste
- 2 thin slices onion, cut in half
- 1 teaspoon whole wheat flour
- Pinch garlic powder
- 1 tablespoon (15 ml) neutral-flavored oil
- ½ teaspoon olive oil
- 8 ounces (227 g) fresh Brussels sprouts, trimmed, rinsed, and thinly sliced

Stir together the mayonnaise, mustard, and lemon juice in a small bowl. Season with salt and pepper, and refrigerate, covered, until using, up to 2 days.

Preheat the oven to 300°F (150°C, or gas mark 2).

Toss the onion slices with the flour, garlic powder, and a pinch of salt and pepper.

Heat the neutral-flavored oil in the wok or skillet over high heat. Test it by adding a piece of onion. If it sizzles, it is ready. Add the onions and cook for 4 to 6 minutes, stirring occasionally. The onions should brown, but not burn. Transfer to a paper towel–lined plate, and blot the excess oil. Keep the onions warm in the oven while preparing the sprouts. Wipe the wok or skillet clean with a paper towel.

Heat the olive oil in the same wok or skillet over high heat. Add the Brussels sprouts and cook for 5 to 7 minutes, stirring occasionally, until desired tenderness. The sprouts will get some black spots. Season with salt and pepper. Transfer the sprouts to a serving plate using a slotted spoon. Sprinkle the onions over the Brussels sprouts, and drizzle with the sauce. Serve immediately.

GLUTEN-FREE
POTENTIAL

SPEARS AND 'SHROOMS

Hearty grilled mushrooms marry well with roasted asparagus, especially when dressed with a marvelous mustard mixture. Choose thinner asparagus spears for this recipe for the very best flavor.

Yield: 4 servings

1 pound (454 g) fresh asparagus, tough ends trimmed

1 medium-size shallot (about 1 ounce, or 30 g), chopped

1 tablespoon (15 ml) fresh lemon juice

1 tablespoon plus 1 teaspoon (20 ml) olive oil, divided

Salt and pepper, to taste

2 portobello mushrooms (8 ounces, or 227 g), stem and gills removed

2 tablespoons (30 ml) white balsamic vinegar

1 tablespoon (15 g) stone-ground mustard

1 teaspoon tamari

1 teaspoon pure maple syrup

Preheat the oven to 400°F (200°C, or gas mark 6).

Combine the asparagus, shallot, lemon juice, and 1 teaspoon oil in a 9 × 13-inch (23 × 33 cm) pan. Add a pinch of salt and pepper, and toss to coat. Roast for 20 minutes, or until tender.

Rub both sides of the mushrooms with the remaining 1 tablespoon (15 ml) olive oil and season with salt and pepper. Heat a grill pan over high heat. Grill the mushrooms for about 5 minutes, or until marked. Turn over to cook the second side until marked, about 5 minutes. The mushrooms should be tender in the center. Slice into ¼-inch (6 mm) strips, and add to the asparagus.

In a small bowl, mix together the vinegar, mustard, tamari, and maple syrup. Pour over the asparagus and mushrooms. Toss to coat, and return to the oven for 5 minutes.

Season to taste with salt and pepper upon serving. Serve hot, warm, or at room temperature.

Stuffed and Dipped

Now's the time for some serious hands-on snacks with off-the-chart fun and flavor factors!

The common denominator for all of the finger foods that follow is that they're packed with fantastic fillings and can be enjoyed with a variety of delightful dips and sassy sauces. It's a pretty straightforward deal, and a delicious one at that!

NACHO SAUCY DIP

Creamy chip sauce without the dairy? *Sí!* As written, the dip is relatively mild, so adjust the seasonings to suit your taste.

Yield: 1¼ cups (310 g)

2 tablespoons (30 ml) olive oil

2 tablespoons (20 g) minced onion

1 tablespoon (10 g) minced scallion

2 cloves garlic, minced

½ teaspoon ground cumin

½ teaspoon smoked paprika

½ teaspoon fine sea salt, more to taste

½ teaspoon chili powder, more to taste (optional)

¼ cup (23 g) oat flour

2 teaspoons pickled jalapeños, minced, more to taste

¾ cup (180 ml) unsweetened plain vegan milk

¼ cup (30 g) nutritional yeast

½ cup (120 g) diced fire-roasted canned tomatoes with adobo or chipotle (not drained)

Heat the olive oil, onion, scallion, garlic, cumin, paprika, salt, and chili powder in a medium-size saucepan over medium heat. Cook, stirring, for 3 to 4 minutes, until fragrant. Whisk in the oat flour, and cook for 3 to 4 minutes longer, until the flour is cooked. Whisk in the jalapeños, milk, and nutritional yeast. Reduce the heat to a simmer.

Cook and whisk until thickened, 6 to 8 minutes. Stir in the tomatoes. The texture of the sauce thickens slightly as it cools to room temperature. Leftovers can be covered and refrigerated for up to 4 days. Reheat gently over medium-low heat, stirring and adding splashes of milk, as needed, to reach the desired consistency.

CHIPOTLE ALMONDS

These almonds go great with beer, but they are just as addictive on long car rides or walks in the woods. Slightly sweet, a little smoky, they take minutes of hands-on time and really deliver on taste.

Yield: 2 cups (280 g)

¼ cup (60 ml) pure maple syrup

2 chipotle peppers in adobo

2 tablespoons (30 ml) olive oil

2 teaspoons onion powder

2 teaspoons ground cumin

1 teaspoon chili powder

1 teaspoon fine sea salt

2 cups (240 g) raw, shelled almonds

Preheat the oven to 325°F (170°C, or gas mark 3). Combine the maple syrup, chipotle peppers, oil, onion powder, cumin, chili powder, and salt in a mini blender. Process until smooth. Pour into a medium-size bowl, and add the almonds. Stir to coat the almonds.

Line a large baking sheet with parchment paper. Spread the nuts on the sheet in a single layer. Bake for 10 minutes, then stir. Bake for 6 to 10 minutes longer, or until the almonds are glazed and lightly toasted, stirring occasionally. The coating will harden as the almonds cool. Break the almonds apart when cool, and store in an airtight container at room temperature for up to 2 weeks.

SAUERKRAUT-STUFFED SEITAN ROUNDS

Our testers found the glaze on these seitan rounds was the ideal finish, but if you like to dip, serve them with Thousand Island Sauce (page 92).

Yield: 48 rounds

4 ounces (113 g) extra-firm tofu, crumbled

½ cup (120 ml) vegetable broth, plus more if needed

2 tablespoons (30 ml) sauerkraut juice from a jar

2 tablespoons (33 g) tomato paste

2 tablespoons plus 1 teaspoon (35 ml) tamari, divided

1½ cups (216 g) vital wheat gluten

¼ cup (30 g) nutritional yeast

1 tablespoon plus 1 teaspoon (8 g) ground coriander

1 tablespoon plus 1 teaspoon (9 g) ground cumin

1 tablespoon plus 1 teaspoon (10 g) onion powder

2 teaspoons smoked paprika

2 teaspoons dried mustard

2 teaspoons garlic powder

1 teaspoon allspice

½ teaspoon ground black pepper

1 cup (142 g) sauerkraut, drained (rinsed if you are salt sensitive)

½ teaspoon caraway seeds

2 teaspoons Dijon mustard

2 teaspoons pure maple syrup

Neutral-flavored oil, for cooking

Prepare a steamer and four 10-inch (25 cm) pieces of foil.

Combine the tofu, broth, sauerkraut juice, tomato paste, and 1 tablespoon (15 ml) tamari in a small blender. Blend until smooth.

Combine the vital wheat gluten, nutritional yeast, and the spices in a medium-size bowl. Pour the wet ingredients into the dry ingredients and stir with a fork until combined. Add 1 tablespoon (15 ml) of broth or (9 g) vital wheat gluten if needed to make a dough. Knead into a cohesive ball. Divide the mixture into 4 equal portions (5½ ounces, or 156 g each) and place on the foil.

Stir together the sauerkraut and caraway seeds in a small bowl.

Shape the dough into a 6-inch (15 cm) log, about 1½ inches (4 cm) in diameter. Using your fingers, press to form a trench down the length of the log. Divide the sauerkraut evenly among the logs. Sprinkle with caraway seeds. Fold the dough to enclose the sauerkraut, pinching to close, and patching with pinches of dough where needed. Roll the foil around the filled dough, and twist the ends. Steam for 1 hour 10 minutes. Let cool, and refrigerate until serving.

Stir together the remaining 1 tablespoon plus 1 teaspoon (20 ml) tamari, mustard, and syrup in a small bowl. Slice the sausages into ½-inch (1.3 cm) rounds. Heat a thin layer of oil in a cast-iron skillet over medium-high heat. Brush one side of the rounds with the tamari mixture and place in the skillet, sauced side down. Brush the tops with the rest of the mixture. Cook for 6 minutes, until browned. Turn over to cook the second side, about 5 minutes. Serve hot or at room temperature with toothpicks.

KIMCHI-STUFFED SAUSAGES

We know how hard it can be to find specialty ingredients. If you aren't able to find the Korean hot pepper powder, substitute cayenne pepper. It won't be the same, but it will still taste great.

Yield: 72 rounds

4 ounces (113 g) extra-firm tofu, drained, crumbled

1¾ cups (396 g) drained kimchi, not squeezed, divided

½ cup (120 ml) water, plus more if needed

3 tablespoons (50 g) organic ketchup

1 tablespoon (15 ml) tamari

2 teaspoons ground coriander

1 teaspoon ground ginger

1 teaspoon ground cumin

1 teaspoon garlic powder

1 teaspoon onion powder

1 teaspoon Korean hot pepper powder

1 teaspoon ground white pepper

1½ cups (216 g) vital wheat gluten

¼ cup (30 g) nutritional yeast

1 tablespoon (15 ml) neutral-flavored oil

Korean sauce from Baked Buffalo Tofu Bites (page 63)

Minced scallion and sesame seeds, for garnish

Combine the tofu, 1 cup (226 g) of the kimchi, water, ketchup, tamari, coriander, ginger, cumin, garlic powder, onion powder, and peppers in a blender. Process until smooth. Whisk together the vital wheat gluten and nutritional yeast in a medium-size bowl. Add the tofu mixture, and stir to combine with a fork. Mix together well. The mixture should be cohesive and able to be formed. Add 1 tablespoon (15 ml) water or (9 g) vital wheat gluten if needed to make a dough.

Prepare a steamer and six 10-inch (25 cm) pieces of foil. Divide the mixture evenly among the foil pieces: each piece will be 4 ounces (113 g). Shape each into a 6-inch (15 cm) log. Make a deep indentation down the center, leaving the ends intact. Fill with a generous 2 tablespoons (28 g) of the remaining kimchi, and pinch closed well. Try to center the filling so the sausages will not tear when cooking. Shape into a sausage and close the foil, twisting the ends. If the log isn't sealed well, the kimchi may fall out when slicing or cooking. Repeat with the remaining sausages, and steam for 1 hour 10 minutes. Refrigerate until serving.

Use a serrated knife to carefully cut the sausages into ½-inch (1.3 cm) rounds. Heat the oil in a large skillet over medium heat. Cooking in batches, cook the sausages until browned, about 4 minutes per side. Turn over to cook the second side, about 3 minutes. Keep warm. When all the sausages are browned, return them to the skillet along with the sauce. Stir to coat, and cook for 1 minute.

Transfer to a plate, and sprinkle with the scallions and sesame seeds.

BAKED BUFFALO TOFU BITES

A finger food book would be sadly lacking if it didn't include a recipe for this traditional "wing-style" dish. Made with tofu, these cubes still cry out for the traditional sides of celery sticks and dip (pictured here with our Pantry Raid Ranch Dip, page 57, and Korean-inspired sauce, recipe below).

Yield: 4 servings

For the bites:

2 tablespoons (30 ml) hot sauce, such as Frank's

2 tablespoons (30 ml) tamari

2 teaspoons Dijon mustard

2 teaspoons onion powder, divided

1 teaspoon garlic powder, divided

¼ teaspoon ground black pepper, plus more to taste

15 ounces (425 g) extra-firm tofu, drained and pressed, cut into 1-inch (2.5 cm) cubes

Nonstick cooking spray

3 tablespoons (45 ml) unsweetened plain vegan milk

½ cup (64 g) arrowroot powder, more if needed

1 cup (80 g) panko crumbs

Salt, to taste

For the sauce:

½ cup (120 ml) hot sauce, such as Frank's

2 tablespoons (28 g) vegan butter, melted

2 teaspoons Dijon mustard

1 teaspoon pure maple syrup

To make the bites: Combine the hot sauce, tamari, mustard, 1 teaspoon of the onion powder, ½ teaspoon of the garlic powder, and pepper in a medium-size bowl. Stir together. Add the tofu, stirring to coat. Cover and refrigerate for a minimum of 1 hour, or up to 12 hours.

Preheat the oven to 400°F (200°C, or gas mark 6). Lightly coat a baking sheet with cooking spray.

Remove the cubes from the marinade, and add the milk to any remaining marinade. Put the arrowroot powder on a plate. Combine the panko, remaining 1 teaspoon onion powder, remaining ½ teaspoon garlic powder, salt, and pepper on a plate. Dip the cubes into the marinade mixture, shaking off any excess, then coat with the arrowroot. Dip them into the marinade mixture again, then generously coat with panko. Place the cubes on the baking sheet, and bake for 25 minutes. Turn over and bake for 10 minutes longer, or until nicely golden.

To make the sauce: Whisk the ingredients together in a medium-size bowl. Serve the cubes with the sauce and toothpicks. For super spicy results, the sauce can be poured over the cubes just before eating.

SERVING SUGGESTIONS & VARIATIONS

Make a Korean-inspired sauce instead! Yield: ¾ cup (180 ml)

3 tablespoons (60 g) Korean red pepper paste

3 tablespoons (45 ml) tamari

3 tablespoons (45 ml) seasoned rice wine vinegar

2 tablespoons (33 g) organic ketchup

½ teaspoon toasted sesame oil

2 scallions, thinly sliced

2 teaspoons toasted sesame seeds

Combine the first five ingredients in a small bowl. Whisk to combine. The sauce may be prepared up to 2 days ahead. To serve, spoon over bites and garnish with the scallions and sesame seeds.

MINI POLENTA ROUNDS

Lightly crusted and full of flavor, these little rounds can be dipped in Nacho Saucy Dip (page 58), if desired, or topped with a bit of salsa. The corn and scallions make them pleasing to the eye, while the Cajun seasoning makes them taste sensational.

Yield: 18 rounds

Nonstick cooking spray

1½ cups (355 ml) vegetable broth

2 cloves garlic, minced

1 teaspoon onion powder

1 teaspoon Cajun seasoning blend

2 teaspoons olive oil

½ cup (70 g) polenta

¼ cup plus 2 tablespoons (60 g) corn kernels

2 tablespoons (20 g) minced scallion

Neutral-flavored oil, for cooking

Lightly coat eighteen cups of a mini muffin pan with cooking spray.

In a pot, heat the broth, garlic, onion powder, Cajun seasoning, and olive oil over high heat until boiling. Slowly add the polenta, corn, and scallion, stirring until combined. Reduce the heat to low and simmer, stirring constantly, for 8 to 10 minutes. The mixture should be very thick. Fill each muffin cup with about 1½ tablespoons (18 g) of the polenta mixture, smoothing the tops. Refrigerate for 1 hour. Or the pan can be covered with plastic wrap and refrigerated for up to 2 days.

Carefully pop the polenta rounds out of the pan. Heat a thin layer of oil in a large skillet over high heat. When the oil ripples, reduce the heat to medium. Cook the rounds in batches, for 3 to 4 minutes, until golden. Carefully turn over to cook the second side until golden, about 3 minutes. The outsides should be slightly crisp. Some of the corn may fall out, but that's okay. The corn also causes the oil to splatter, so be careful. Blot the excess oil with a paper towel, if desired, and serve hot with toothpicks.

MOROCCAN SNACK BARS

We've all eaten (and loved) sweet snack bars, but now it's time for a savory bar to take its place at the table! We've packed these with traditional North African flavors, to create a super flavorful finger food. Harissa brands vary in heat, so add it to your own taste.

Yield: 20 bars

Nonstick cooking spray

½ cup (87 g) dry Israeli couscous

1 cup (235 ml) vegetable broth

1 teaspoon fine sea salt, divided

Scant 1 cup (90 g) cauliflower florets, divided

Scant ¼ cup (25 g) sliced carrot (about 1 carrot)

¾ cup (197 g) cooked Great Northern beans

¼ cup (40 g) minced red onion

Juice from ½ fresh lemon

2 teaspoons ground cumin

1 teaspoon ground coriander

¼ teaspoon ground white pepper

2 cloves garlic, minced

1 teaspoon harissa, or to taste

1 teaspoon minced fresh ginger

½ cup (63 g) all-purpose flour

½ cup (54 g) slivered almonds, roughly chopped

⅛ teaspoon smoked paprika

Preheat the oven to 375°F (190°C, or gas mark 5). Lightly coat an 8-inch (20 cm) square baking pan with cooking spray.

Cook the couscous with the broth and ½ teaspoon of the salt according to package directions. Set aside.

Combine ½ cup (45 g) of the cauliflower and the carrot in a food processor. Process until minced. Transfer to a medium-size bowl. Put the remaining ½ cup (45 g) cauliflower in the food processor, and pulse a few times to make smaller florets. Add to the bowl. Put the beans in the processor, and pulse a few times to break the beans down, but do not form a paste. Add the beans to the bowl along with the remaining ½ teaspoon salt, onion, lemon juice, cumin, coriander, pepper, garlic, harissa, and ginger. Mix well. Mix in the flour.

Pack the mixture into the prepared pan, and top evenly with the almonds. Gently press the almonds into the mixture. Sprinkle with the smoked paprika. Bake for 40 minutes, until the almonds are beginning to turn golden. Let cool before cutting. Serve at room temperature. The bars can be made up to 2 days in advance, then covered and refrigerated.

> **RECIPE NOTE**
>
> Harissa is a very flavorful, hot pepper paste originally from Tunisia. Its popularity is spreading throughout the world. Different regions, even different households, have their own unique versions. There are recipes online and in other cookbooks if you wish to make your own, or the paste can be found in the ethnic food aisle of well-stocked grocery or specialty stores.

MEDITERRANEAN MEATLESS BALLS

This tofu-based appetizer can be a show-stealer. With such a large amount of fresh basil, it's no surprise. Add the olives and sun-dried tomatoes, and a star is born! We'd be remiss if we didn't mention that our testers suggested eating these on sandwiches with Quickie Marinara (page 16).

Yield: 14 to 16 balls

¼ cup (40 g) pitted kalamata olives

¼ cup (16 g) soft sun-dried tomato halves (not oil-packed)

½ cup (12 g) packed fresh basil

8 ounces (227 g) extra-firm tofu, drained, pressed, and crumbled

¼ cup (40 g) finely minced onion

3 tablespoons (28 g) minced green bell pepper

2 tablespoons (30 ml) fresh lemon juice

2 tablespoons (15 g) nutritional yeast

2 cloves garlic, minced

½ teaspoon dried thyme

½ teaspoon dried oregano

½ teaspoon fine sea salt

¼ teaspoon ground black pepper

Pinch red pepper flakes

¼ cup (66 g) tomato paste, more if needed

½ cup (63 g) all-purpose flour, divided

Nonstick cooking spray

Neutral-flavored oil, for cooking

Quickie Marinara (page 16) or Tomato-Thyme Gravy (page 47), heated, for serving

Combine the olives and sun-dried tomatoes in a small blender. Process until finely chopped. Add the basil, and process until combined. Put the tofu in a medium-size bowl, and add the basil mixture, mashing the tofu with a fork and mixing together. Stir in the onion, pepper, lemon juice, nutritional yeast, garlic, thyme, oregano, salt, pepper, and red pepper flakes until well combined. Mix with your hands, if necessary, to make a uniform mixture. Stir in the tomato paste and ¼ cup (31 g) of the flour. The mixture should be shapeable. If it isn't, add 1 tablespoon (17 g) extra tomato paste, and stir again. Lightly coat a baking sheet with cooking spray.

For baking: Preheat the oven to 325°F (170°C, or gas mark 3). Scoop 1 tablespoon (25 g) of the mixture, and form a ball. Place the ball on the sheet. Repeat until all the mixture is used. Lightly coat the balls with cooking spray. Bake for 20 minutes, until lightly browned. Turn over carefully, and spray again. Bake for 20 minutes longer, until golden. Broil the balls for 5 minutes.

For panfrying: Place the remaining ¼ cup (31 g) flour on a plate. Scoop 1 tablespoon (25 g) of the mixture, and form a ball. Roll the ball in the flour, and place the ball on the sheet. Repeat until all the mixture is used. Heat a thin layer of oil in a large skillet over medium heat. Line a plate with a paper towel for draining. Fry the balls for 8 to 10 minutes, turning occasionally, until golden. Drain briefly on the paper towel–lined plate.

Serve the balls hot, warm, or at room temperature with the sauce and toothpicks.

RECIPE NOTE

Only ¼ cup (31 g) of flour is required for this recipe if you choose to bake it rather than panfry it.

JAMAICAN JERK TEMPEH SKEWERS

As written, this is a very mild jerk sauce. Sweet pineapple and brilliant red bell peppers make for a gorgeous presentation. For more heat, use the full jalapeño or a different type of hot pepper, such as the traditional Scotch bonnet.

Yield: 32 toothpicks

For the sauce:

½ cup (120 ml) vegetable broth

2 scallions, trimmed

1 tablespoon (17 g) tomato paste

1 tablespoon (15 ml) apple cider vinegar

2 teaspoons pure maple syrup

2 teaspoons olive oil

½ jalapeño pepper, stemmed and seeded, more to taste (see headnote)

3 cloves garlic, minced

One ½-inch (1.3 cm) round of fresh ginger, peeled

½ teaspoon fine sea salt

½ teaspoon dried thyme

½ teaspoon sweet paprika

½ teaspoon ground cumin

¼ teaspoon ground allspice

¼ teaspoon ground black pepper

8 ounces (227 g) tempeh, steamed, cut into 1-inch (2.5 cm) cubes

For the skewers:

32 toothpicks

Two ½-inch (1.3 cm) round slices red onion, each cut into 16 pieces

Four ½-inch (1.3 cm) round slices fresh pineapple, each cut into 8 pieces

2 medium-size red bell peppers, each cut into sixteen 1-inch (2.5 cm) pieces

Nonstick cooking spray

To make the sauce: Combine all the ingredients in a blender and process until smooth. Place the tempeh cubes in a 9-inch (23 cm) square baking dish. Pour the sauce over the tempeh cubes and toss to coat. Cover and refrigerate for at least 24 hours or up to 3 days, turning occasionally.

To make the skewers: With a toothpick, skewer a piece of onion, a tempeh cube (letting the extra sauce drip back into the dish), a piece of pineapple, and a piece of bell pepper on each of thirty-two toothpicks.

Heat a grill pan over high heat. Lightly coat the grill pan with cooking spray.

Transfer the toothpicks to the grill pan, and cook until marked, about 5 minutes, while basting with the remaining jerk sauce. Turn to cook the second side until marked, about 5 minutes, still basting. Serve hot, warm, or at room temperature.

BANH MI LETTUCE WRAPS

Banh mi sandwiches are one of our favorites. We couldn't resist coming up with a finger food version. Fresh and full of tasty crunch, these can be spiced to your preference.

The sausages used in this recipe are the Kimchi-Stuffed Sausages (page 60), but made a little differently. Omit the filling and shape the sausages into four portions (each about 7 ounces, or 192 g). Use the sausages after steaming. Freeze three of the sausages for future use, or try them in any Asian-style dish.

Yield: 36 to 45 small wraps, 2½ cups (340 g) filling

2 teaspoons neutral-flavored oil

½ teaspoon toasted sesame oil

1 sausage (page 60), diced (see headnote)

1 tablespoon (15 ml) tamari

1 cup (76 g) minced Napa cabbage

2 tablespoons (20 g) minced red onion

2 tablespoons (14 g) grated carrot

¼ to ⅓ cup (56 to 74 g) vegan mayonnaise, to taste

2 teaspoons fresh lime juice

½ teaspoon Sriracha, or to taste

½ cup (52 g) mung bean sprouts, chopped

1 tablespoon (1 g) minced fresh cilantro (optional)

12 to 15 romaine lettuce leaves

4-inch (10 cm) piece of cucumber, peeled if desired, sliced, and cut into quarters

Heat the oils in a large skillet over medium-high heat. Add the sausage and cook, stirring, for 4 to 5 minutes, until browned. Turn the heat off, and add the tamari, stirring to coat. Set aside to let cool.

Combine the cabbage, onion, carrot, mayonnaise, lime juice, and Sriracha in a medium-size bowl. Stir in the sausage when it is cool. This mixture can be covered and refrigerated for up to 24 hours. When serving, stir in the bean sprouts and cilantro, and taste to adjust the seasonings. Spoon 3 to 4 tablespoons (27 to 36 g) of the mixture onto each lettuce leaf. The amount will depend on the size of the romaine leaves. Cut the leaves into three or four pieces, depending on the length of the leaves. Top each with a few cucumber quarters.

POT STICKERS

We love five-spice powder. We love tempeh. Put them in a wrapper, and we'll think it's a present any time!
No bow needed, but the dipping sauce is another story.

Yield: 24 pot stickers

For the dipping sauce:

3 tablespoons (45 ml) tamari

1 tablespoon (15 ml) seasoned rice vinegar

¼ teaspoon Sriracha, to taste

For the pot stickers:

4 ounces (113 g) tempeh, steamed, finely minced

1½ tablespoons (23 ml) tamari

¼ teaspoon Chinese five-spice powder

1 tablespoon (15 ml) neutral-flavored oil, plus extra for panfrying the pot stickers

1 teaspoon toasted sesame oil

2 cloves garlic, minced

½ teaspoon minced fresh ginger

⅛ teaspoon ground white pepper

1 cup (76 g) minced Napa cabbage

2 tablespoons (20 g) minced scallion, plus more for garnish

24 vegan wonton wrappers

½ cup (120 ml) vegetable broth, divided

To make the dipping sauce: Stir together all the ingredients in a small bowl. Set aside until serving. The sauce can be made ahead, covered, and refrigerated for up to 4 days.

To make the pot stickers: Combine the tempeh with the tamari and five-spice powder. Marinate for 1 hour at room temperature, or up to 8 hours if stored in the refrigerator. Heat the oils in a large skillet over medium heat. Add the tempeh, garlic, ginger, and white pepper. Cook, stirring occasionally, for 6 to 8 minutes, until deeper brown. Transfer to a medium-size bowl, and let cool. Stir in the cabbage and scallion. Taste and adjust the seasonings. This can be made ahead of time and stored in the refrigerator for up to 24 hours.

Working in batches of six, spread the wonton wrappers on a work surface. Keep a small bowl of water nearby. Put about 2 teaspoons of filling in each of the wonton wrappers. Dip your fingers in the water, and pat them on two consecutive sides of the inside of the wrappers. Fold the top over, sealing well with your fingers. Cover with a damp towel while assembling the rest.

Preheat the oven to 300°F (150°C, or gas mark 2).

Heat a thin layer of oil in a large skillet over medium heat. Cook the pot stickers in batches, and do not crowd them in the skillet. Cook for 3 to 5 minutes, or until the edges and bottom are golden. Turn over to cook the second side, 2 to 4 minutes, or until golden. Turn the heat off and pour 2 tablespoons (30 ml) of broth into the skillet. Let cook in the residual heat until evaporated. Put the pot stickers on a plate, and keep warm in the oven. Wipe the skillet with a paper towel, and cook the remaining pot stickers in the same manner. Garnish with scallions if desired, and serve with the sauce for dipping.

BAKED FRITTATA MINIS

Broccoli and pasta in a frittata? Yes, please! Feel free to serve the red sauce with other recipes in this book, such as the Mini Polenta Rounds (page 64), but especially with the Sambusas (page 94).

For the red sauce:

¾ cup (135 g) chopped tomato

⅓ cup (49 g) chopped red bell pepper

3 tablespoons (30 g) chopped shallot

2 cloves garlic, minced

1 teaspoon minced fresh ginger

1 teaspoon olive oil

¼ teaspoon ground cinnamon

¼ teaspoon cayenne pepper, more to taste

1 tablespoon (15 ml) red wine vinegar

1 tablespoon (15 ml) water, more if needed

Salt and pepper, to taste

For the frittata minis:

Nonstick cooking spray

1 ounce (28 g) dry capellini or angel hair noodles, broken into 1-inch (2.5 cm) pieces

2 teaspoons olive oil

1 cup (91 g) minced broccoli

¼ cup (40 g) minced onion

2 tablespoons (8 g) soft sun-dried tomato halves (not oil-packed), minced

¼ teaspoon dried dill

2 cloves garlic, minced

Salt and pepper, to taste

10 ounces (283 g) extra-firm tofu, drained and crumbled

¼ cup (60 ml) unsweetened plain vegan milk

1 tablespoon plus 1 teaspoon (11 g) nutritional yeast

1 tablespoon plus 1 teaspoon (20 ml) fresh lemon juice

1 tablespoon (15 ml) ume plum vinegar

Yield: 22 mini frittatas, ¾ cup (142 g) sauce

To make the red sauce: Combine all the ingredients in a small skillet. Bring to a boil, then reduce to a simmer. Cook for 10 minutes, stirring occasionally. Remove from the heat and process in a blender until smooth. Let the flavors meld for at least 30 minutes. The sauce can be covered and refrigerated for up to 3 days. Taste and adjust the seasonings when serving. Serve at room temperature.

To make the frittata minis: Preheat the oven to 400°F (200°C, or gas mark 6). Lightly coat twenty-two cups of a mini muffin pan with cooking spray.

Cook the noodles according to the package directions, and drain.

Heat the oil, broccoli, onion, sun-dried tomatoes, and dill in a large skillet over medium heat. Cook, stirring occasionally, until the broccoli is bright green, about 3 minutes. Remove from the heat and stir in the garlic. Season to taste with salt and pepper.

Combine the tofu, milk, nutritional yeast, lemon juice, and vinegar in a blender. Process until smooth. Pour into the broccoli mixture and add the noodles. Stir to combine. Scoop by 1 tablespoon (20 g), and drop in the muffin cups. Pat the tops smooth. Continue until all the tofu mixture has been used.

Bake for 25 to 30 minutes, until the tops are slightly golden and firm to the touch. Remove from the tin and serve hot, warm, or at room temperature.

FALAFEL FRITTERS WITH SPICY TAHINI SAUCE

These are more falafel than not, but we chose to call them fritters to be just a bit more accurate. They are still full of the falafel flavors you know and love. Our cashew-based tahini sauce is spiked with harissa (a North-African chili sauce) and is the perfect partner. If you happen to have extra dipping sauce, try it as a salad dressing.

Yield: 18 falafel, ¾ cup (140 g) sauce

For the spicy tahini sauce:

¼ cup (35 g) raw cashews

3 tablespoons (45 ml) vegetable broth

2 tablespoons (32 g) tahini

2 tablespoons (30 ml) seasoned rice vinegar

1 tablespoon (15 ml) fresh lemon juice

2 cloves garlic, minced

1 teaspoon harissa, or more to taste

½ teaspoon fine sea salt

For the falafel:

1 can (15 ounces, or 425 g) chickpeas, drained and rinsed

¼ cup (40 g) finely minced red onion

3 tablespoons (28 g) finely minced green bell pepper

2 tablespoons (30 ml) fresh lemon juice

1 tablespoon (4 g) finely minced fresh parsley

2 cloves garlic, minced

1 teaspoon ground cumin

1 teaspoon ground coriander

½ teaspoon fine sea salt

½ teaspoon ground white pepper

¼ cup (31 g) all-purpose flour

High-heat neutral-flavored oil, for cooking

To make the spicy tahini sauce: Combine all the ingredients in a small, high-powered blender. Process until completely smooth. Taste and adjust the seasonings. Serve immediately, or cover and refrigerate for up to 4 days.

To make the falafel: Put the chickpeas in a food processor and process until crumbly, but not a paste. Transfer to a medium-size bowl and add the onion, pepper, lemon juice, parsley, garlic, cumin, coriander, salt, and pepper. Stir to combine, then use your hands to mash a little. Add the flour, and mix together. The mixture should hold its shape. If not, add a bit more flour. Using a slightly heaping tablespoon (20 g), shape into 18 small flat rounds, about 1 inch (2.5 cm) in diameter.

Heat a thin layer of oil in a large skillet over medium-high heat. Cook the falafel until lightly browned, about 4 minutes. Turn over to cook the second side until golden, about 4 minutes. Drain on a plate lined with paper towels. Serve hot, warm, or at room temperature.

PULLED JACKFRUIT MINI TACOS

Tacos are the ultimate folded-type of finger food! These are packed with a super flavorful combination of an almost stew-like, smoky shredded jackfruit filling and topped with creamy guacamole and zesty salsa fresca.

Yield: 12 tacos

- 1 tablespoon (15 ml) liquid smoke
- 1 tablespoon (15 ml) tamari
- 1 tablespoon (15 ml) pure maple syrup
- 1 teaspoon garlic powder
- 1 teaspoon onion powder
- ⅛ to ¼ teaspoon ground black pepper, to taste
- ⅛ to ¼ teaspoon cayenne pepper, to taste
- ⅛ teaspoon dried oregano or ¼ teaspoon dried basil
- ¼ teaspoon Citrus Thyme Salt (page 24), fine sea salt, or celery salt
- 3 sprigs fresh thyme
- 1 can (20 ounces, or 565 g) jackfruit in brine or water (not syrup), rinsed, drained, and lightly squeezed to remove excess water
- ¾ cup (180 ml) vegetable broth
- 1 tablespoon (15 ml) olive oil
- 7 ounces (200 g) diced celery and carrot mix
- 1 shallot, minced
- 2 cloves garlic, minced
- 12 6-inch (15 cm) corn or flour tortillas
- Guacamole (page 118), to taste
- Salsa fresca, to taste

Combine the liquid smoke, tamari, maple syrup, garlic powder, onion powder, peppers, oregano, salt, fresh thyme, jackfruit, and broth in a 10-inch (25 cm) baking dish with a lid.

Place the oil in a skillet. Sauté the celery and carrot mix, shallot, and garlic over medium heat until the veggies just start to get tender, about 6 minutes. Stir the sautéed veggies into the baking dish with the jackfruit. Cover and marinate overnight in the refrigerator.

Preheat the oven to 325°F (170°C, or gas mark 3). Place the baking dish in the oven, and cook for 1 hour. Remove the cover and stir; use two forks to shred the jackfruit, and cook uncovered until the liquid is absorbed, about 30 minutes. Remove from the oven, and discard the thyme sprigs. Adjust the seasonings if needed. Keep warm while heating the tortillas.

Heat a dry skillet over medium heat. Place a tortilla in the pan and heat until warm and soft, about 30 seconds on each side.

Fill each tortilla with ¼ cup (40 g) of the warm pulled jackfruit and top with guacamole and salsa fresca, to taste. Fold closed, and serve immediately.

BAKED LENTEJA TAQUITOS

The next time you cook lentils (*lenteja* in Spanish) and make mashed potatoes, be sure to keep enough to make these crispy taquitos. The filling can be prepared the day before, so that all you have to do on the day of your party (or as a simple snack attack) is roll these up, bake, and enjoy them.

Yield: 24 taquitos

1 tablespoon (15 ml) olive oil

¼ cup (40 g) chopped onion

2 cloves garlic, minced

1 tablespoon (8 g) mild to medium chili powder

1½ teaspoons ground cumin

1 teaspoon smoked paprika

¼ to ½ teaspoon cayenne pepper, to taste

3 tablespoons (50 g) organic ketchup or tomato paste

1 cup (235 ml) unsweetened plain vegan milk

¼ cup plus 2 tablespoons (48 g) nutritional yeast

½ teaspoon fine sea salt

1½ tablespoons (23 ml) apple cider vinegar

1 tablespoon (16 g) tahini

1 teaspoon dried cilantro or
1 tablespoon (1 g) chopped fresh cilantro (optional)

¾ cup (158 g) mashed potatoes

2 cups (330 g) cooked green lentils (al dente)

24 6-inch (15 cm) corn tortillas, heated to soften if needed

Nonstick cooking spray or olive oil, for brushing

Green salsa or salsa fresca, for serving

Place the oil and the onion in a heavy-bottomed, large saucepan, and heat over medium-high. Cook the onion until softened, about 2 minutes. Lower the heat to medium and add the garlic, chili powder, cumin, paprika, and cayenne pepper; cook and stir for 1 minute. Add the ketchup, stirring to combine; cook for 1 minute. Add the milk, nutritional yeast, salt, vinegar, tahini, cilantro, and mashed potatoes. Stir to combine. Add the lentils, and simmer for 8 minutes, or until thickened. Let cool for about an hour or overnight in the refrigerator before assembling the taquitos.

Preheat the oven to 400°F (200°C, or gas mark 6). Have two large baking sheets handy. Spread 2 tablespoons (35 g) filling in the center of the tortilla, and roll tightly, being careful not to squeeze the filling out from either end. Repeat with the remaining tortillas. Coat with cooking spray on both sides, or generously brush with olive oil.

Place the taquitos on the baking sheets, 12 per sheet, seam-side down. Bake for 15 to 20 minutes, until golden brown and crispy. Check after 10 minutes, and if you see the taquitos are threatening to crack, carefully remove the sheet from the oven and lightly coat the taquitos with cooking spray, or brush with oil again. Serve hot with green salsa or salsa fresca.

MEAN BEAN TACO CUPS

We fell in love with this method of making tortilla cups. Give it a try, and we know you will, too. They are versatile, so let your ideas run wild. Shake up the seasoning on them, and then concoct your own filling. (But try our version first, of course.)

Yield: 12 cups

3 8-inch (20 cm) flour tortillas

Nonstick cooking spray

½ teaspoon smoked salt

½ cup (86 g) cooked black beans

½ cup (52 g) minced cucumber

1 tablespoon (9 g) minced red or yellow bell pepper

1 tablespoon (10 g) finely minced red onion

1 teaspoon minced fresh cilantro, or more to taste

½ teaspoon chipotle in adobo sauce, or more to taste

1 tablespoon (15 ml) red wine vinegar

Salt and pepper, to taste

½ avocado, pitted, peeled, and diced

Juice from ½ fresh lemon

Preheat the oven to 400°F (200°C, or gas mark 6).

Using a 3-inch (8 cm) round cutter, cut 4 rounds from each tortilla. Lightly coat one side of each small round with cooking spray and sprinkle evenly with smoked salt. Using two 12-cup inverted regular muffin pans, tuck a round (salted side up) in between 4 of the cups, curving the sides up to form a small bowl. Repeat until all the rounds are used. Bake for 6 minutes, or until the edges are lightly browned. Cool on a wire rack. The bowls can be stored in an airtight container for up to 3 days before using.

Combine the beans, cucumber, bell pepper, onion, and cilantro in a small bowl.

With a mortar and pestle, pound the chipotle into the vinegar until smooth. Pour over the bean mixture, stirring to coat. Taste and adjust the seasonings. Spoon about 1 tablespoon (12 g) into each cup. Toss the avocado with the lemon juice, and season with salt and pepper. Sprinkle a few pieces on each cup. Serve immediately.

SERVING SUGGESTION & VARIATION

For spicier tastes, add 1 tablespoon (9 g) minced jalapeño to the bean mixture.

RECIPE NOTE

The rest of the tortillas can be cut into strips, lightly coated with cooking spray, placed on a baking sheet, and baked as above. Use them instead of croutons on salads or soups.

RED PEPPER HUMMUS TARTLETS

One of our favorite ways to flavor (and color) hummus is to add roasted red bell peppers, so that's what we chose as a filling for these fancy little savory tartlets, but you can use any favorite hummus in its place, including our Smoked Chickpea Hummus (page 20), and garnish it to your liking.

Yield: 10 tartlets

For the filling:

1 can (15 ounces, or 425 g) chickpeas, drained and rinsed

¼ roasted red bell pepper (about 1 ounce, or 28 g)

2 cloves garlic, minced

1 tablespoon (9 g) capers with brine, plus extra for garnish

1 tablespoon (4 g) soft sun-dried tomato halves (not oil-packed)

¼ to ½ teaspoon red pepper flakes, to taste

2 tablespoons (30 ml) extra-virgin olive oil

1 tablespoon (15 ml) fresh lemon juice

For the crusts:

Nonstick cooking spray

1¼ cups (150 g) whole wheat pastry flour

½ teaspoon fine sea salt

2 teaspoons evaporated cane juice (see Glossary, page 11)

¼ cup (60 ml) olive oil or neutral-flavored oil

⅓ cup (80 ml) cold unsweetened plain vegan milk, as needed

Chopped fresh basil or parsley, for garnish

To make the filling: Combine all the ingredients in a food processor, and pulse a few times. Stop the food processor, scrape down the sides with a rubber spatula, and process until just slightly chunky. Place in an airtight container in the refrigerator and chill for a couple of hours or overnight to let the flavors meld.

To make the crusts: Preheat the oven to 350°F (180°C, or gas mark 4). Lightly coat ten 3-inch (8-cm) quiche or tart pans with cooking spray.

Place the flour, salt, sugar, and oil in a food processor. Pulse a few times to combine. Add the milk as needed, 1 tablespoon (15 ml) at a time, until the crumbs of dough are moist enough to stick together easily when pinched. Fill each prepared pan with 1 heaping tablespoon (24 g) of the dough, and press down firmly starting at the bottom, then sliding upward to cover the edges. Bake for 16 minutes, or until light golden brown around the top edges. Let the pans cool for 15 minutes, and carefully remove the crusts from the pans to cool completely on a wire rack.

Place 2 tablespoons (38 g) of filling per cooled crust, and use an offset spatula to smooth the top. Decorate the tops with capers and fresh herbs, if desired. Serve immediately or place in the refrigerator until ready to eat. It's best to fill the crusts only when ready to eat, or up to 2 hours prior.

Store the filling leftovers in an airtight container in the refrigerator for up to 4 days, and leftover crusts in an airtight container at room temperature for up to 2 days.

CREAMY LEEK MINI PIES

If you've made Celine's Papet Vaudois (a Swiss potato and leek kind of stew) from *The Complete Guide to Vegan Food Substitutions*, then you'll find that the flavor of the creamy filling in these wee little pies bears a strong resemblance to it. It's bound to be love at first bite!

Yield: 24 mini pies

For the filling:

1 cup (260 g) Cashew Almond Spread (page 121)

1 or 2 cloves garlic, to taste

¼ teaspoon Citrus Thyme Salt (page 24) or fine sea salt

2 tablespoons (6 g) minced fresh chives

1 tablespoon (4 g) minced fresh parsley

¾ teaspoon onion powder

7 ounces (200 g) trimmed leeks, chopped small, thoroughly washed, and drained

½ cup (120 ml) vegetable broth

2 tablespoons (30 g) mild Dijon mustard

Salt and pepper, to taste

For the crusts:

Nonstick cooking spray

1½ cups (180 g) whole wheat pastry flour

Scant ½ teaspoon Rosemary Orange Salt (page 24) or fine sea salt

3 tablespoons (45 ml) neutral-flavored oil

¼ cup plus 2 tablespoons (90 ml) cold unsweetened plain vegan milk, as needed

To make the filling: Combine the spread, 1 clove garlic, salt, chives, parsley, and onion powder in a food processor. Process until completely smooth, adjust the quantity of the garlic and salt to your taste.

Combine the leeks, broth, and mustard in a medium-size pot. Bring to a boil, lower the heat, cover with a lid, and simmer until tender, about 8 minutes. Stir the spread into the leeks until combined; remove from the heat. Season with salt and pepper to taste, and set aside.

To make the crusts: Preheat the oven to 350°F (180°C, or gas mark 4). Lightly coat a 24-cup mini muffin pan with cooking spray. Place the flour, salt, and oil in a food processor. Pulse a few times to combine. Add 2 tablespoons (30 ml) of the milk, pulse to combine, then add the remaining ¼ cup (60 ml) milk as needed, 1 tablespoon (15 ml) at a time, until the crumbs of dough stick together easily when pinched. Place a generous 1½ teaspoons of crumbs in each muffin cup, pressing down to fit the bottom and sides of the cup.

Add 2 generous teaspoons of filling per crust, smoothing out the tops. There will be a little less than ¼ cup (75 g) leftover filling, which is delicious served at room temperature or even cold on bread. (Store leftovers in the refrigerator in an airtight container if not using straightaway.)

Bake for 22 minutes, or until the tops are firm and light golden brown. Remove from the pan, transfer to a wire rack, and serve warm or at room temperature. Leftovers can be stored in an airtight container in the refrigerator for up to 2 days and reheated in a 325°F (170°C, or gas mark 3) oven until warm, about 15 minutes.

TINY TOMATO PIES

A crisp whole-grain crust, packed with a spinach, basil, and tofu filling, all topped with a cherry ... cherry tomato, that is. These little pies fly off the table at any gathering.

Yield: 24 mini pies

For the crusts:

Nonstick cooking spray

2 cups (240 g) whole wheat pastry flour

½ teaspoon fine sea salt

¼ cup plus 2 tablespoons (90 ml) olive oil

¼ cup plus 2 tablespoons (90 ml) cold water

For the filling:

½ cup (20 g) packed spinach leaves

¼ cup (10 g) packed basil leaves

2 tablespoons (18 g) raw cashews

2 tablespoons (20 g) chopped onion

1 tablespoon plus 1 teaspoon (11 g) nutritional yeast

Juice from 1 fresh lemon

8 ounces (227 g) extra-firm tofu, drained, pressed, and crumbled

½ cup (120 ml) unsweetened plain vegan milk

½ teaspoon fine sea salt

Pinch ground black pepper

12 cherry tomatoes, halved

Preheat the oven to 400°F (200°C, or gas mark 6). Lightly coat a 24-cup mini muffin pan with cooking spray.

To make the crusts: Stir the flour and salt together in a medium-size bowl. Drizzle in the oil, and stir with a fork to create crumbs. Add the water 1 tablespoon (15 ml) at a time, stirring with the fork, until it forms a dough. Scoop a generous 2 teaspoons of dough and form into a ball. Put in one of the muffin cups, and press to line the whole cup. Repeat until all the dough has been used.

To make the filling: Put the spinach, basil, and cashews in a small food processor. Process until finely chopped. Add the onion, nutritional yeast, and lemon juice, and pulse again. Add the tofu, milk, salt, and pepper. Process until smooth. Fill each cup with about 2 teaspoons filling, using all the filling. Top each with a cherry tomato half cut-side down, and bake for 25 to 30 minutes. The tops will be golden brown, and the crusts should be done. Serve hot or at room temperature.

ANTIPASTA TOFU-STUFFED SHELLS

The tofu is seasoned with a perennial vegan favorite, nutritional yeast, as well as other goodies, before being combined with roasted asparagus and flavorful artichoke hearts to make an incredible variation on a tofu salad. We couldn't resist adding peppery arugula (ever!) to really take this over the top. Stuff it in a pasta shell, and you've got a fabulous finger food.

Yield: 14 to 18 shells

Nonstick cooking spray

1 tablespoon (8 g) nutritional yeast

1 tablespoon (15 ml) tamari

1 tablespoon (15 ml) olive oil

1 tablespoon (15 ml) liquid smoke

1 tablespoon (15 ml) vegan dry red wine

½ teaspoon pure maple syrup

½ teaspoon garlic powder

Salt and pepper, to taste

1 pound (454 g) extra-firm tofu, drained, pressed, and cut into ¼-inch (6 mm) cubes

6 stalks roasted asparagus, cut into ¼-inch (6 mm) pieces

3 tablespoons (30 g) minced scallion

4 artichoke hearts, minced

2 tablespoons (8 g) soft sun-dried tomato halves (not oil-packed)

1 tablespoon (9 g) capers, drained and minced

1 cup (40 g) packed baby arugula, minced

¼ cup (11 g) chopped fresh basil

2 tablespoons (30 ml) red wine vinegar

Pinch red pepper flakes

2 tablespoons (28 g) vegan mayonnaise, or more to taste

14 to 18 dry, jumbo, vegan pasta shells, cooked al dente, drained

Preheat the oven to 400°F (200°C, or gas mark 6). Lightly coat a large rimmed baking sheet with cooking spray.

In a medium-size bowl, stir together the nutritional yeast, tamari, oil, liquid smoke, wine, syrup, garlic powder, and generous pinches of salt and pepper. Stir in the tofu to coat. Spread the tofu on the sheet and bake for 30 to 35 minutes, until golden and firm in texture. Let cool.

Stir together the tofu, asparagus, scallion, artichoke hearts, sun-dried tomatoes, capers, arugula, basil, vinegar, red pepper flakes, and mayonnaise. Taste and adjust the seasonings. If desired, the filling can be made ahead of time and stored in an airtight container in the refrigerator for up to 2 days. Moisten it with extra mayonnaise if needed when assembling.

Fill each shell with about 2 tablespoons (34 g) filling. Serve at room temperature.

BAKED POLENTA FRIES WITH AVOCADO DIP

Making your own polenta fries from scratch might take a smidge longer than purchasing a tub of premade polenta from the store does, but the main advantage is that you get to season them as you wish. Be prepared to see everyone, including young children (these were kid approved!), go gaga for these.

Yield: Approximately 64 fries, heaping 1¼ cups (273 g) dip

For the fries:

2 cups (470 ml) unsweetened plain vegan milk

2 cups (470 ml) vegetable broth

2 tablespoons (15 g) nutritional yeast

Heaping ½ teaspoon Citrus Thyme Salt (page 24) or fine sea salt, plus extra

2 cloves garlic, pressed

2 cups (240 g) medium-grind cornmeal (preferably organic)

2 tablespoons (15 g) corn flour (not cornstarch, preferably organic)

Nonstick cooking spray

Up to ¼ cup (60 ml) olive oil, plus more for greasing the sheet

To make the fries: Combine the milk, broth, nutritional yeast, salt, and garlic in a large saucepan and bring to a boil. Lower the heat, then slowly stream in the cornmeal and corn flour, whisking constantly. Reduce the heat to medium low. Using a wooden spoon, stir almost constantly and cook for 15 minutes, or until the polenta is so thick that when you slash a line through its center with the spoon the line remains and the polenta doesn't fill in the slash. Note that cooking times will vary depending on the type of cornmeal you use, so watch for cooking cues. Be sure to adjust the temperature if needed, to avoid scorching. Remove from the heat.

Lightly coat an 8-inch (20 cm) square baking pan with cooking spray, and spread the polenta evenly in the prepared pan, using an angled spatula. Do not cover the pan.

Once cooled to room temperature, cover the pan and place it in the refrigerator for at least 2 hours, and up to overnight.

Preheat the oven to 425°F (220°C, or gas mark 7). Lightly brush a large rimmed baking sheet with olive oil.

Remove the chilled polenta from the pan, and cut it into ½-inch (1.3 cm) strips, flipping the strips on the side (they will be approximately 1-inch [2.5 cm] wide once flipped) and cutting them lengthwise in half again to obtain two ½-inch (1.3 cm) wide, 8-inch (20 cm) long strips, then cut both once in the middle widthwise. You should get fries of approximately 4 × ½ inch (10 × 1.3 cm); lightly brush the fries with oil, and space them evenly on the prepared sheet. Feel free to lightly salt your fries before baking.

Bake for 20 minutes, flip the fries, and bake for another 15 to 20 minutes, or until golden brown and crispy. While the fries are baking, prepare the dip.

For the dip:

1 large or 2 small ripe avocados, pitted and peeled

1 tablespoon (15 ml) fresh lemon or lime juice

¼ cup (60 g) unsweetened plain vegan yogurt or (56 g) vegan mayonnaise

2 tablespoons (20 g) chopped red onion

2 tablespoons (8 g) fresh parsley leaves

1 or 2 cloves garlic, pressed, to taste

¼ teaspoon ground cumin

Salt and pepper, to taste

To make the dip: Place all the ingredients in a food processor; pulse just to combine, stopping to scrape down the sides once with a rubber spatula, and turn into a somewhat chunky dip. Remove from the food processor and store in an airtight container in the refrigerator until serving. Best served within a day or two, so that the avocado doesn't get a chance to oxidize.

RECIPE NOTES

- To make the fries in portions rather than all at once, keep uncut leftovers wrapped tightly in the refrigerator for up to 3 days. Bake when desired.

- If you like a lot of dip with your fries, the avocado dip recipe can be easily doubled.

PAD THAI SUMMER ROLLS

While they look beautiful and seem difficult to make, summer rolls are actually quite simple! The spring roll wrappers are nearly translucent, so make the most of it by topping the roll with a sprig of cilantro. It's the ideal accent for our pad Thai–inspired filling.

Yield: 8 summer rolls

For the tofu:

3 tablespoons (45 ml) tamari, divided

1 tablespoon (15 ml) toasted sesame oil

1 tablespoon (15 ml) pure maple syrup

½ teaspoon onion powder

½ teaspoon garlic powder

½ teaspoon ground ginger

8 ounces (227 g) extra-firm tofu, drained, pressed, and cut into ¼-inch (6 mm) slices

1 tablespoon (15 ml) neutral-flavored oil

For the rolls:

1 cup (104 g) chopped cucumber

¼ cup plus 2 tablespoons (42 g) grated carrot

¼ cup plus 2 tablespoons (60 g) minced scallion

2 tablespoons (30 ml) seasoned rice vinegar

Eight 8-inch (20 cm) spring roll wrappers

8 fresh cilantro leaves

½ cup (52 g) mung bean sprouts

1 generous handful dry rice sticks, cooked al dente

For the sauce:

2 tablespoons (32 g) natural creamy peanut butter

2 tablespoons (30 ml) tamari

2 tablespoons (30 ml) seasoned rice vinegar

Preheat the oven to 400°F (200°C, or gas mark 6).

To make the tofu: Combine 2 tablespoons (30 ml) tamari, sesame oil, maple syrup, onion and garlic powders, and ginger in an 8-inch (20 cm) square baking dish. Add the tofu, turning to coat. Bake for 15 minutes. Turn over and bake for 15 minutes longer. The tofu should be browned. This can be made ahead of time and refrigerated until assembling, up to 3 days.

When assembling the rolls, cut the baked tofu slices into ¼-inch (6 mm) sticks. Heat the oil in a medium-size skillet over medium heat. Cook the tofu for 4 to 5 minutes, until crisp. Add the remaining 1 tablespoon (15 ml) tamari, and stir and cook for 3 to 5 minutes, until the tofu is coated and the tamari is absorbed.

To make the rolls: Combine the cucumber, carrot, scallion, and vinegar in a small bowl. Soak one wrapper according to the package directions. Place a cilantro leaf in the center of the wrapper, add about 2 tablespoons (26 g) of the cucumber mixture, four to five pieces of tofu, eight to ten mung bean sprouts, and one-eighth of the rice sticks. Fold the top and bottom ends of the wrapper in and roll across the wrapper to make an eggroll shape. Continue with the remaining ingredients, until all eight rolls have been prepared.

To make the sauce: Whisk all the ingredients together in a small bowl. Serve with the rolls.

SUSHI RICE ROLLS

Our testers ran into the same issue we did when preparing these: It's hard to quit snacking on the rice and tempeh while assembling the rolls! Just try to reserve enough of each component to get a reasonable amount of food to serve your guests. (At the very least, be sure to have a fridge packed with veggie sticks, chips, and dips in case you didn't manage to show restraint.)

Yield: 16 rolls, 1 cup (224 g) sushi sauce

For the rice:

1 cup (208 g) uncooked sushi rice, thoroughly rinsed and drained

1¼ cups (295 ml) water

1 tablespoon (15 ml) fresh lemon juice

1 teaspoon toasted sesame oil

1 teaspoon Sriracha

1 teaspoon tamari

1 teaspoon light agave nectar or brown rice syrup

1 tablespoon (8 g) black sesame seeds

For the tempeh:

8 ounces (227 g) tempeh

Nonstick cooking spray

2 tablespoons (30 ml) tamari

1 or 2 cloves garlic, pressed, to taste

2 tablespoons (30 ml) seasoned rice vinegar

1 teaspoon ground ginger

To make the rice: Combine the rice and water in a rice cooker, cover with the lid, and cook until the water is absorbed without lifting the lid.

While the rice is cooking, combine all the remaining ingredients in a large bowl.

Let the rice sit for 10 minutes in the rice cooker with the lid on. Gently fold the cooked rice into the dressing, and let cool before using. If preparing this step the day before serving, cover and store in the refrigerator until ready to use.

To make the tempeh: Lightly coat the uncut block of tempeh with cooking spray. Place in a hot skillet, lower the heat to medium, and brown the block until dark golden brown, about 5 minutes on each side. Remove from the heat, place on a wire rack, and let cool for a few minutes. Combine the remaining ingredients in a medium-size bowl. Cut the tempeh into ½-inch (1.3 cm) cubes, add to the marinade, and fold to coat. Refrigerate for 1 hour, or up to overnight.

To make the sushi sauce: Combine the mayonnaise, Sriracha, and oil in a medium-size bowl. Cover and refrigerate until serving.

Immerse the spring roll wrappers 1 sheet at a time in warm water to soften. Soak for a few seconds, until pliable. Handle carefully because the wraps tear easily. Drain on a clean kitchen towel before rolling.

For the sushi sauce:

1 cup (224 g) vegan mayonnaise

1 tablespoon (15 ml) Sriracha, more if desired

1 teaspoon toasted sesame oil

16 8-inch (20 cm) spring roll wrappers

32 thin, 3-inch (8 cm) long red bell pepper sticks

32 thin, 3-inch (8 cm) long cucumber sticks

To assemble, place two packed tablespoons (30 g) of rice per moistened wrapper. Place three tempeh cubes on top of the rice, one pepper stick on each side (two in all) of the rice/tempeh mound, and one cucumber stick on each side (two in all) of the rice/tempeh mound. Use the vegetable sticks to grab onto as you roll the rolls tightly. Repeat with the remaining rolls until you run out of one or all of the ingredients. Cover with plastic wrap and refrigerate until serving. Be careful when separating the rolls: the wraps might stick to each other a little, but won't tear if you separate them slowly. The rolls will keep for up to 2 days, stored covered in the refrigerator.

RECIPE NOTES

- It's best to have a few extra spring roll wrappers handy in case the ones you use are a little brittle and could use doubling.

- If you don't have a rice cooker, use your preferred method of cooking rice, and follow the instructions on the package of rice to obtain the best results.

- If you don't have vegan mayonnaise at home and want to make something that's a good stand-in for it, here's how. Blend together (in a food processor or blender) until perfectly smooth 12 ounces (340 g) soft or firm silken tofu, ¼ cup (60 ml) neutral-flavored oil, 2 tablespoons (30 ml) fresh lemon juice, and ½ teaspoon fine sea salt. Optional add-ins: 1 or 2 cloves garlic and freshly ground black pepper to taste. Store in an airtight container in the refrigerator for up to 1 week.

ROASTED EGGPLANT BREAD SPREAD

We love the rustic simplicity of this spread. But if you'd like to dress it up a little, stir in 2 tablespoons (8 g) soft sun-dried tomato halves (not oil-packed), minced, or (13 g) minced black olives right before serving.

Yield: 1½ cups (276 g)

Nonstick cooking spray

1 medium eggplant (a little under 14 ounces, or 385 g), trimmed, peeled, and cut into 1-inch (2.5 cm) cubes

3 leeks, white parts only, about 4 inches (10 cm) long, thoroughly cleaned, sliced in half lengthwise

4 marinated artichoke hearts, drained

2 tablespoons (30 ml) olive oil

Salt and pepper, to taste

3 cloves garlic

1 tablespoon (15 ml) fresh lemon juice

Preheat the oven to 400°F (200°C, or gas mark 6). Lightly coat a large rimmed baking sheet with cooking spray.

Put the eggplant, leeks, and artichoke hearts on the baking sheet. Toss with the oil and season with salt and pepper. Roast for 10 minutes, stir, and add the garlic cloves. Roast for 15 minutes longer. The vegetables should begin to look a little brown in spots. Remove the garlic cloves, and transfer the vegetables to a food processor. Mince the garlic and add it and the lemon juice to the food processor. Pulse a few times to create a chunky spread. Season to taste with salt and pepper. Serve warm or at room temperature. The spread can be made ahead, covered, and stored in the refrigerator for up to 2 days. Bring the spread to room temperature for serving.

SMOKY FOUR-SEED CRACKERS

We love to enjoy these in their "naked" form, but we support you if you're more of a must-have-a-dip kind of snack eater. In which case, we recommend you pair them with our Cashew Almond Spread (page 121), our Smoked Chickpea Hummus (page 20), or any spread or dip that doesn't have too bold a flavor that would end up masking the terrific personality of these crackers. We love making a batch of these and serving them alongside our Green Snackers (page 99).

Yield: Approximately 150 small crackers

2 tablespoons (30 ml) neutral-flavored oil

1 tablespoon (15 ml) liquid smoke

2 teaspoons pure maple syrup

2 teaspoons apple cider vinegar

1 teaspoon smoked paprika

1 teaspoon onion powder

¾ teaspoon fine sea salt

1½ cups (180 g) whole wheat pastry flour

1 tablespoon (9 g) white sesame seeds

1 tablespoon (8 g) golden roasted flaxseeds

1 tablespoon (9 g) poppy seeds

1 tablespoon (15 g) chia seeds

½ cup (120 ml) cold water, as needed

RECIPE NOTE

These crackers will also be great if you prefer switching the seeds used here to those you love most or whatever is available in your refrigerator or pantry.

Preheat the oven to 350°F (180°C, or gas mark 4). Have two baking sheets handy.

In a small bowl, combine the oil, liquid smoke, maple syrup, and vinegar.

In the bowl of a stand mixer fitted with the paddle attachment, combine the paprika, onion powder, salt, flour, and all the seeds. Add the oil mixture to the dry ingredients. Mix on medium speed, and add the water slowly, until a dough forms without being too dry or too wet. You should only need ⅓ cup (80 ml) water, but add the remainder if needed. Divide the dough in half.

Using a rolling pin, roll out each piece of dough on a separate piece of parchment paper or silicone baking mat, as thinly and evenly as you can, approximately ⅛-inch (3 mm) thick. Cut into approximately 1-inch (2.5 cm) square crackers, using a pastry wheel. The crackers don't need to be separated once cut. Just transfer each piece of parchment paper or baking mat to a baking sheet.

Bake for 14 to 16 minutes, or until the crackers look dry and are fragrant. Check occasionally to make sure the edges don't get too brown. If some crackers bake faster than others, carefully remove them and place on a wire rack.

Transfer to a wire rack. Store in an airtight container once cooled, for up to 4 days.

GREEN SNACKERS

Flaky and crisp, these crackers are a welcome addition to any get-together. As a bonus, they're even popular with kids! Take note: The thinner the dough is rolled, the crisper the crackers will be. We serve them with our Smoky Four-Seed Crackers (page 97, see photo at left).

Yield: 24 to 28 crackers

¾ cup (90 g) whole wheat pastry flour

¼ cup (31 g) all-purpose flour

½ teaspoon fine sea salt

Pinch ground black pepper

2 tablespoons (28 g) vegan butter

1 cup (40 g) packed fresh spinach

¼ cup (60 ml) cold water

Preheat the oven to 375°F (190°C, or gas mark 5).

In a medium-size bowl, whisk together the flours, salt, and pepper. Cut in the butter to resemble small peas.

Combine the spinach and water in a mini blender. Process until smooth. Pour into the flour mixture and stir to combine with a fork. If the mixture is too wet or dry, add additional flour or water 1 teaspoon at a time. The mixture should form a ball.

Lightly flour a work surface, and roll the dough out to between ⅛- (3 mm) and ¼-inch (6 mm) thick. Using a 2-inch (5 cm) round cutter, cut the dough into crackers. Transfer to a baking sheet, and poke each cracker twice with a fork. Bake for 20 to 24 minutes (for biscuit-like crackers) or 24 to 28 minutes (for crisp crackers), until firm and the bottoms are starting to brown. Transfer to a wire rack. Store in an airtight container once cooled, for up to 4 days.

FRY-ANYTHING DOUGH

This dough is so versatile! We use it in both sweet and savory recipes in this book, and encourage you to develop your own variations. Just be sure to seal it well after filling. It's used in our Sambusas (page 94), Traditional Eggless Rolls (page 93), and the Eggless Roll Smash-Ups (page 92). And don't miss the Sweet Pecan Triangles (page 150)!

Yield: About 11 ounces (325 g), enough for about twenty 3-inch (8 cm) squares or eight 6-inch (16 cm) squares

1 cup (125 g) all-purpose flour, plus more as needed

½ cup (70 g) whole spelt flour

½ teaspoon fine sea salt

1 tablespoon (15 ml) olive oil

½ cup (120 ml) water, plus more as needed

Combine the flours and salt in a medium-size bowl. Stir together with a fork. Add the oil, and stir in. Add the water and mix with the fork. It should form a slightly wet but not sticky dough. Add an extra 1 tablespoon (15 ml) of water if too dry or 1 tablespoon (8 g) all-purpose flour if too wet. Cover and let sit at room temperature for 1 hour before using, or cover and refrigerate for up to 2 days. Let the dough come to room temperature before using as directed in specific recipes.

SALSA SCUFFINS

Part muffin, part scone, these are delicious plain, but feel free to dip them in Nacho Saucy Dip (page 58), Guacamole (page 118), or Rasta Salsa (page 16). If you like heat, the spicier the salsa, the better these are!

Yield: 14 scuffins

Nonstick cooking spray

¾ cup (90 g) whole wheat pastry flour

½ cup (70 g) whole spelt flour

1 teaspoon baking powder

1 teaspoon cornstarch

1 teaspoon Sucanat

½ teaspoon Smoked Paprika Salt (page 24) or fine sea salt

½ teaspoon ground cumin

3 tablespoons (45 ml) olive oil

½ cup (152 g) jarred salsa, drained (reserve the liquid)

Unsweetened plain vegan milk, as needed

1 tablespoon (9 g) finely minced jalapeño pepper, more if desired (optional)

Preheat the oven to 375°F (190°C, or gas mark 5). Lightly coat a mini muffin pan (about 14 cups) with cooking spray.

Stir together the flours, baking powder, cornstarch, Sucanat, salt, and cumin in a medium-size bowl. Drizzle in the olive oil, and stir with a fork until the mixture resembles crumbs. Starting with the liquid from the salsa, add enough milk to make ½ cup (120 ml) total liquid. Add the salsa, jalapeño, and liquid to the bowl and stir to combine, but do not overstir. Spoon a heaping 1½ tablespoons (about 30 g) batter into each cup.

Bake 20 to 24 minutes, until lightly browned. Serve hot or at room temperature.

MINI SAVORY SCONES

Although these scones may be on the smaller side, they sure pack a serious flavor punch! Some of our testers enjoyed munching on them with a bowl of extra Cashew Almond Spread (page 121) on the side, sprinkled with a little extra salt. We love them on their own, but they would also be fantastic served with our Quickie Marinara (page 16), Mediterranean Meatless Balls (page 66), and Mediterranean Stuffed Mushrooms (page 28), for example.

Yield: 27 mini scones

- 2 cups (240 g) whole wheat pastry flour
- 1 tablespoon (12 g) baking powder
- ¾ teaspoon Smoked Paprika Salt (page 24) or fine sea salt
- 2 teaspoons mild to medium chili powder
- 2 teaspoons onion powder
- 3 large cloves garlic, minced
- 2 tablespoons (8 g) soft sun-dried tomato halves (not oil-packed)
- ½ cup (130 g) Cashew Almond Spread (page 121)
- 2 tablespoons (30 ml) neutral-flavored oil
- 3 tablespoons (45 ml) unsweetened plain vegan milk, more if needed

Preheat the oven to 375°F (190°C, or gas mark 5). Line two baking sheets with parchment paper or silicone baking mats.

Place the flour, baking powder, salt, chili powder, onion powder, minced garlic, and sun-dried tomatoes in a food processor. Pulse a couple of times to mince the tomatoes and combine. Add the cashew almond spread and oil and pulse to combine. Scrape down the sides with a rubber spatula if needed. Add the milk and pulse to combine. The dough crumbs should hold together well when pinched. If the mixture is crumbly, add extra milk 1 teaspoon at a time, pulsing to combine.

Pack 1 tablespoon (20 g) with dough crumbs to make one scone. Place on the prepared sheet, and flatten just slightly. Repeat with the remaining dough. You should get twenty-seven scones in all.

Bake for 14 minutes, or until golden brown on the bottom. Transfer to a wire rack.

Store leftovers in an airtight container for up to 2 days, but keep in mind these are best enjoyed fresh.

SERVING SUGGESTIONS & VARIATIONS

These scones are also great made with a heaping ¾ cup (130 g) of just-ripe avocado slices, to replace the Cashew Almond Spread. Avoid using an overly ripe avocado because it imparts too strong a flavor. Use a food processor to blend the avocado briefly but thoroughly so no large chunks are left.

LEMON-FENNEL SCONE BITES

These flaky, savory bites are so perfect when enjoyed straight from the oven that we feel they don't need anything to accompany them. But if you really must, they will pair beautifully with any of our small plate vegetable recipes, such as Green Beans Jalfrezi and Tahini Cauliflower (page 49), or with trays of homemade or store-bought vegan cheeses.

Yield: 16 small scones

1½ cups (180 g) whole wheat pastry flour

2 teaspoons baking powder

Generous ½ teaspoon fine sea salt

2 tablespoons (24 g) Sucanat

½ cup (128 g) tahini or other nut or seed butter

¼ cup (60 ml) fresh lemon juice

Zest from 1 organic lemon

2 small cloves garlic, minced

2 teaspoons fennel seeds

¼ cup (60 ml) plain unsweetened vegan milk, more if needed

Preheat the oven to 400°F (200°C, or gas mark 6). Line a baking sheet with parchment paper or a silicone baking mat.

In a food processor, combine the flour, baking powder, salt, and Sucanat. Add the tahini, and pulse a few times to combine. Add the lemon juice, zest, garlic, and fennel seeds, and pulse a few times. Add the milk through the hole in the lid, 1 tablespoon (15 ml) at a time, while pulsing until a dough ball forms. It should be moist, but not too wet to handle. If it does crumble, you'll need to pulse a little more milk (1 teaspoon at a time) into it. Place the dough on another piece of parchment paper or a silicone baking mat, and pat it down to a little over ½-inch (1.3 cm) thickness. (Using a rolling pin would make for tough scones, so avoid it.)

Use a 2-inch (5 cm) biscuit cutter to cut the dough into scones and place them on the prepared baking sheet. Gather the scraps of dough and repeat the process until no dough is left. You should get approximately 16 scones.

Bake for 12 to 14 minutes, or until golden brown around the edges on the bottom, and light golden on top. Remove from the oven and let cool on a wire rack.

Store leftovers in an airtight container for up to 2 days. Toast slightly before enjoying the leftovers.

SERVING SUGGESTIONS & VARIATIONS

If you're not a fan of the licorice-like flavor of fennel seeds, you can replace them with the same amount of cumin seeds.

GREEN MONSTER BREAD, REVISITED

We love this bread from *Vegan Sandwiches Save the Day!* so much that we had to make it again. This version is a pot-baked round and can be served with any of the spreads or dips in this book, or on its own. It's that good.

Yield: 1 round loaf

1 cup (60 g) packed fresh kale or (40 g) fresh spinach

1 tablespoon (9 g) minced garlic

1¼ cups (295 ml) water, lukewarm

1 tablespoon (15 ml) olive oil

½ cups (180 g) white whole wheat flour

1¼ cups (156 g) all-purpose flour

½ cup (70 g) whole spelt flour

1½ teaspoons fine sea salt

1 teaspoon instant yeast

Put the kale, garlic, water, and oil in a blender; blend until smooth.

In a large bowl, combine the flours, salt, and yeast. Add the wet ingredients and mix with a wooden spoon only until all the flour is moistened. It will be a thick dough and should stick to the spoon as a ball. Cover loosely and let sit at room temperature for 4 hours. Cover with plastic wrap and refrigerate for 12 to 48 hours.

Line a 2-quart (2 L) bowl with a tea towel. This is a wet dough, so use floured hands. Dust the dough with flour. Loosely shape it into a ball, and place in the towel-lined bowl. Dust with flour again, and cover with plastic wrap. Let rise in a warm place for 1 to 1½ hours, until the indentation of a finger poked into the dough doesn't fill in.

When the dough is nearly risen, put a heavy enamel or cast-iron 2-quart (2 L) covered casserole pot in the oven. Make sure the handle of the pot is oven-safe. Preheat the oven to 475°F (240°C, or gas mark 9).

When the dough is ready, remove the pot carefully. With floured hands (remember it is a wet dough), gather the dough and transfer to the pot. Gently shake so the dough fills the bottom of the pot. Cover and bake for 15 minutes. Uncover and bake for another 15 minutes, until the bread is golden and has pulled from the sides of the pot. The bread is done when it sounds hollow when tapped on the bottom with your knuckles. Cool completely on a wire rack before slicing.

PULL-APART PESTO BREAD

This is the kind of fun bread you have to dig into and tear apart to enjoy. We love to serve it with Roasted Eggplant Bread Spread (page 96), Quickie Marinara (page 16), or extra pesto!

Yield: 1 loaf

....

1 cup (235 ml) water

½ cup (80 g) steel-cut oats

½ cup (120 ml) plain vegan milk, warm

2 tablespoons (30 ml) olive oil

2 tablespoons (30 ml) brown rice syrup or light agave nectar

2½ cups (300 g) white or regular whole wheat flour

2 tablespoons (18 g) vital wheat gluten

2¼ teaspoons instant yeast

1 teaspoon fine sea salt

Nonstick cooking spray

½ cup (118 g) vegan pesto (double recipe in Eggplant Stackers, page 122)

Bring the water and oats to a boil in a small saucepan. Lower the heat to a simmer, and cook for 8 minutes, stirring occasionally. The mixture will be rather thick. Set aside to cool to lukewarm. Stir in the milk, olive oil, and syrup.

In the bowl of a stand mixer fitted with a dough hook, combine the flour, gluten, yeast, and salt. Add the wet ingredients to the dry, and knead for 10 minutes. (Alternatively, knead by hand on a lightly floured surface for 10 minutes.) Add extra flour as needed, until the dough is manageable, pliable, and not too sticky. Cover with plastic wrap and let rise for 90 minutes, or until doubled in size.

Lightly coat an 8 × 4-inch (20 × 10 cm) loaf pan with cooking spray.

Punch down the dough, and roll it out on a lightly floured surface into a 9 × 12-inch (23 × 30 cm) rectangle; spread pesto evenly on the surface.

Using a sharp knife, cut the rolled-out dough lengthwise into six 1½-inch (4 cm) wide strips. Place the strips on top of each other, with the pesto side facing up. Cut into six stacks, each one made of six layers. Transfer the stacks carefully to the prepared pan; it doesn't matter if the stacks don't all fit in a row. Arrange the stacks cut edges up, so it looks like stripes. Cover with plastic, and let rise for 1 hour, or until doubled in size.

Preheat the oven to 375°F (190°C, or gas mark 5). Lower the oven rack so that the bread isn't too close to the heat element. Remove the plastic wrap and lightly coat the top of the bread with cooking spray. Bake for 25 minutes, then loosely cover with a piece of foil and bake for another 15 minutes, or until golden brown.

Remove from the pan, and let cool for at least 15 minutes before diving in. Best served fresh.

TWISTED BREAD STICKS

It's true, we love the extra flavor that beer brings to bread dough. Adding fermented foods or beverages to dishes almost always boosts the taste, and it is no exception here. Serve these with Quickie Marinara (page 16) for dipping.

Yield: 20 bread sticks

....

1 cup (235 ml) flat vegan beer, at room temperature

1 teaspoon light agave nectar

2¼ teaspoons active dry yeast

5 tablespoons (75 ml) olive oil, divided

2 cups (240 g) white or regular whole wheat flour

1 cup minus 1½ teaspoons (120 g) all-purpose flour

½ teaspoon fine sea salt

Nonstick cooking spray

2 teaspoons garlic salt, or more to taste

Combine the beer, agave, and yeast in the mixing bowl of a stand mixer fitted with a dough hook. Stir and let sit for 5 minutes for the yeast to get bubbly. Add 2 tablespoons (30 ml) of the oil, the flours, and the sea salt. Knead for 6 to 8 minutes, until a smooth, cohesive dough is formed. (Alternatively, knead by hand on a lightly floured surface for 10 minutes.) Add an extra 1 tablespoon (15 ml) beer or water or (8 g) flour if needed. Shape the dough into a ball.

Lightly coat a medium-size bowl with cooking spray. Put the dough in the bowl, and turn over so the oiled side is up. Cover with plastic wrap and let rise in a warm place until doubled, about 1½ hours.

Combine the garlic salt and the remaining 3 tablespoons (45 ml) oil. Lightly coat two baking sheets with cooking spray. Lightly flour a work surface. Roll the dough out to an 8 × 15-inch (20 × 38 cm) rectangle. Cut into ten 1½-inch (4 cm) strips. Brush with about 1 tablespoon (15 ml) of the oil mixture. Twist both ends of the dough in opposite directions to form a rope. The rope should be about ½ inch (1.3 cm) thick. Cut in half to make two sticks, and place on the baking sheet. Continue until all the sticks are formed, placing them about 2 inches (5 cm) apart. Brush with another 1 tablespoon (15 ml) of the remaining oil mixture, and let rise for about 30 minutes, until puffy.

Preheat the oven to 400°F (200°C, or gas mark 6). Bake for 13 to 16 minutes, until golden brown. Brush with the remaining 1 tablespoon (15 ml) oil. Serve warm or at room temperature.

RECIPE NOTE

For up-to-date news on which beers (and other liquors) are vegan, be sure to check www.barnivore.com.

SPINACH SWIRLS

These easy little spinach bites are an impressive part of an appetizer spread. Try to resist eating the filling with a spoon, but we won't blame you if you do. Serve these with our Quickie Marinara (page 16).

Yield: 20 swirls

For the dough:

½ cup (120 ml) warm water

1 teaspoon Sucanat

1 teaspoon active dry yeast

1 cup (120 g) white or regular whole wheat flour

½ cup (63 g) all-purpose flour

2 tablespoons (30 ml) olive oil

½ teaspoon Italian herb blend

½ teaspoon fine sea salt

Nonstick cooking spray

For the filling:

3 cups (90 g) finely chopped spinach

2 tablespoons (15 g) nutritional yeast

1 tablespoon (15 ml) olive oil

¼ teaspoon ground black pepper

To make the dough: Stir together the water, Sucanat, and yeast in the mixing bowl of a stand mixer fitted with a dough hook. Stir and let sit for 5 minutes, until the yeast bubbles. Add the flours, oil, Italian herb blend, and salt. Mix on low until the dough forms a smooth ball, about 6 minutes. (Alternatively, knead by hand on a lightly floured surface for 10 minutes.) Add an extra 1 tablespoon (8 g) flour or (15 ml) water if needed to make a cohesive dough. Coat a large bowl with cooking spray. Round the dough into a ball and place it in the bowl, turning so the oiled side is up. Cover with plastic wrap and let rise until doubled, about 1½ hours.

Lightly dust a work surface with flour. Divide the dough in half and roll each half into an 8 × 10-inch (20 × 25 cm) rectangle.

Preheat the oven to 375°F (190°C, or gas mark 5).

To make the filling: Stir together the spinach, nutritional yeast, oil, and pepper in a medium-size bowl. Spread half the filling evenly on each rectangle. Roll from the 10-inch (25 cm) side, pinching the dough together as you go, including the ends and the last edge of the dough, so the swirls don't unwind in the oven. Cut each roll into 1-inch (2.5 cm) slices, and place on a baking sheet with the filling side on top, and against the baking sheet.

Bake the rolls for 18 to 22 minutes, until lightly browned and the centers are cooked. Serve hot, warm, or at room temperature.

X'S AND O'S FOCACCIA

We love the bold look of (asparagus) x's and (onion) o's on this focaccia, but you can chop the vegetables and spread them over the crust if you prefer. Whoever you are serving it to will still feel the love.

Yield: 6 large pieces

For the bread:

1 cup plus 2 tablespoons (265 ml) warm water

1 teaspoon pure maple syrup

2¼ teaspoons active dry yeast

2 cups (250 g) all-purpose flour

1 cup (120 g) white or regular whole wheat flour

2 tablespoons (30 ml) olive oil

1 teaspoon fine sea salt

Nonstick cooking spray

For the topping:

⅓ cup (80 ml) olive oil, plus more for the pan

3 tablespoons (45 g) roasted garlic (see Recipe Note)

2 tablespoons (15 g) nutritional yeast

½ teaspoon Italian herb blend

½ teaspoon fine sea salt

¼ teaspoon ground black pepper

12 pieces (3-inches, or 8 cm, long) asparagus

6 thin rounds red onion

6 thin rounds red bell pepper

To make the bread: Combine the water, maple syrup, and yeast in the bowl of a stand mixer fitted with a dough hook. Let sit for 5 minutes until the yeast is bubbly. Add the flours, oil, and salt. Knead for 5 to 7 minutes, until the dough is silky and smooth. (Alternatively, knead by hand on a lightly floured surface for 10 minutes.) Add an extra 1 tablespoon (15 ml) water or (8 g) flour if needed to make the dough cohesive. Shape the dough into a ball. Lightly coat a medium-size bowl with cooking spray. Put the dough into the bowl, turning so the oiled side is up. Cover with plastic wrap, and let rise in a warm place until doubled in size, about 1 hour.

To make the topping: Combine the oil, garlic, nutritional yeast, herb blend, salt, and pepper in a mini blender. Blend until smooth. Brush a 9 × 13-inch (23 × 33 cm) rimmed baking sheet with oil. Punch down the dough gently, then spread it evenly in the pan. It should fill the pan, stretching into the corners. Spread the oil mixture evenly over the dough, then place the asparagus in an × shape in two rows of three. Place an onion ring on top, then the pepper ring. Gently press the vegetables into the dough. Let rise in a warm place for 30 minutes.

Preheat the oven to 425°F (220°C, or gas mark 7). Bake for 22 to 25 minutes, until golden. Serve hot or at room temperature.

RECIPE NOTE

To roast garlic, preheat the oven to 400°F (200°C, or gas mark 6). Cut back the tops of 3 heads of garlic, and place them on a piece of foil, cupping the foil to hold them upright. Add a pinch of salt and pepper and 1 teaspoon olive oil. Wrap tightly and roast for 40 minutes. The garlic should be golden brown.

MUSHROOM TOASTIES

The creamy mushroom filling contrasts with the crisp grilled bread to make this comfort food appetizer a fast favorite, both in preparation and in how quickly they will disappear!

Yield: 16 mini sandwiches

1 teaspoon olive oil

1 tablespoon (10 g) finely minced shallot

8 ounces (227 g) mushrooms, minced

¼ teaspoon dried thyme

1 teaspoon vegan dry white wine

1 teaspoon vegan Worcestershire sauce

Salt and pepper, to taste

¼ cup (60 g) vegan cream cheese, at room temperature

1 tablespoon (14 g) vegan mayonnaise

2 teaspoons minced fresh chives

½ teaspoon minced fresh thyme

½ teaspoon fresh lemon juice

½ teaspoon Dijon mustard

8 slices bread (¼-inch, or 6 mm, thick), 4 × 5 inches (10 × 13 cm) in diameter

2 tablespoons (28 g) vegan butter, at room temperature

Heat the oil, shallot, mushrooms, and dried thyme in a large skillet over medium heat. Cook, stirring, for 3 to 5 minutes. The mushrooms should look moist, but not release much moisture. Remove from the heat, and stir in the wine and Worcestershire sauce. Season to taste with salt and pepper.

Whisk together the cream cheese, mayonnaise, chives, fresh thyme, lemon juice, and mustard in a small bowl. Spread one side of the bread slices with a thin layer of butter.

Turn them over so the butter side is facing down. Spread 2 teaspoons of the cream cheese mixture on four of the slices of bread. Using a slotted spoon, divide the mushrooms among the four slices with the cream cheese, using about 3 table-spoons (42 g) on each. Put the remaining four slices of bread on top, butter-side out.

Heat a large skillet over medium heat. Toast the sandwiches until golden, about 4 minutes. Turn over to toast the second side for about 3 minutes, until golden. Cut the sandwiches into quarters, using as serrated knife. Serve promptly.

SERVING SUGGESTIONS & VARIATIONS

Substitute an equal amount of Cashew Almond Spread (page 121) for the cream cheese, if desired.

RECIPE NOTE

The yield will vary slightly depending on the dimensions of your bread slices.

HOT PEPPER TOASTWICHES

This is a twist on the popular cream cheese and pepper jelly appetizer, but made so much better because it's layered inside of French toast! With a crisp crust and a creamy middle, this is a sweet and savory way to jump-start your taste buds. Whole wheat French bread and whole wheat pastry flour may be substituted, if desired.

Yield: 32 mini sandwiches

- 3 tablespoons (45 g) vegan cream cheese or Cashew Almond Spread (page 121)
- 16 slices (½-inch, or 1.3 cm, thick) stale French bread
- 3 tablespoons (60 g) hot pepper jelly
- 1 tart apple, cored, cut into thin slices
- 1½ cups (355 ml) unsweetened vegan milk, plus more if needed
- 2 teaspoons apple cider vinegar
- 1 tablespoon plus 1 teaspoon (10 g) nutritional yeast
- 1 tablespoon plus 1 teaspoon (16 g) Sucanat
- ¼ teaspoon ground cinnamon
- 1½ cups (188 g) all-purpose flour
- 2 teaspoons baking powder
- High-heat neutral-flavored oil, for cooking
- 1 to 2 tablespoons (20 to 40 g) blackberry or other jam
- ¼ cup (60 ml) pure maple syrup, for serving

Spread a generous 2 teaspoons of cream cheese on half of the bread slices, followed by a generous 2 teaspoons of hot pepper jelly. Top with two or three apple slices and the remaining slices of bread.

Combine the milk and vinegar in a large shallow baking dish. With a fork, stir in the nutritional yeast, Sucanat, and cinnamon. Stir in the flour and the baking powder. The batter should be thick. Lumps are okay. Add 1 tablespoon (8 g) extra flour if needed to thicken the batter or 1 tablespoon (15 ml) milk to thin it.

Heat ¼ inch (6 mm) of oil in a large skillet over medium-high heat. When it starts to ripple, reduce the heat to medium. Cooking in batches, dip the sandwiches in the batter, turning to coat them completely. Cook the sandwiches for 3 to 4 minutes until the bottoms are golden brown. Turn over to cook the second side until golden. With tongs, turn the slices so that the filled edges of the bread also cook. The whole slice should be golden brown. Cut into halves to serve.

Whisk the jam into the maple syrup, and serve on the side for dipping.

PORTOBELLO HORSERADISH BRUSCHETTA

One of the most popular finger foods ever (according to our not-so-scientific studies)—bruschetta—gets a makeover in this recipe. The traditional tomatoes have vanished. Our seasoned bread is topped with horseradish- and arugula-spiked mayonnaise and grilled-to-perfection portobellos.

Yield: 20 slices

For the bread:

3 tablespoons (45 ml) olive oil

1 teaspoon garlic salt

¼ teaspoon lemon pepper

¼ teaspoon ground black pepper

1 baguette, cut into ½-inch (1.3 cm) slices (about 20 pieces)

For the dressing:

½ cup (112 g) vegan mayonnaise

½ teaspoon (up to 1 teaspoon) prepared horseradish, to taste

¼ cup (5 g) fresh baby arugula, minced

Salt and pepper, to taste

For the portobellos:

¼ cup (60 ml) dry red wine

1 tablespoon (15 ml) tamari

1 tablespoon (15 ml) fresh lemon juice

1 teaspoon Dijon mustard

¼ teaspoon liquid smoke

¼ teaspoon herbes de Provence

4 large portobello mushroom caps, stemmed, gills removed

1 tablespoon (15 ml) olive oil

Large handful pea shoots

To make the bread: Preheat the oven to 400°F (200°C, or gas mark 6). Stir together the oil, garlic salt, lemon pepper, and black pepper in a small bowl. Brush the mixture on one side of each slice of bread, and place on a baking sheet, oil-side up. Bake for 12 to 15 minutes, until golden brown. Remove and let cool on a wire rack. Once cool, the slices can be stored in an airtight container for up to 2 days before using.

To make the dressing: Stir together the mayonnaise, horseradish, and arugula in a bowl. Season with salt and pepper to taste. The sauce can be stored in the refrigerator in an airtight container for up to 24 hours.

To make the portobellos: Combine the wine, tamari, lemon juice, mustard, liquid smoke, and herbes de Provence in a 9 × 13-inch (23 × 33 cm) glass dish. Add the mushroom caps, and turn to coat. Let marinate for 30 minutes.

Heat a grill pan over high heat. Brush the mushrooms with the oil right before cooking. Cook the mushrooms for 3 to 5 minutes, or until grill marks are visible, brushing with the remaining marinade as they cook. Turn over to cook the second side in the same way, about 3 minutes. Transfer to a cutting board, and slice into ½-inch (1.3 cm) strips.

To assemble, taste the mayonnaise mixture, and adjust the seasonings if needed. Spread the mayonnaise evenly on the toasted slices. Divide the pea shoots on top of the slices, and top with the mushroom slices. Serve immediately.

PORTOBELLO BLTS

We don't like to pick favorites, and we're not saying this is one. At least not straight out. We've spread toasted bread slices with creamy, spicy (if you choose) guacamole, and topped it with smoky, crisp vegan bacon to create this open-faced appetizer. We love each of the parts of this recipe, but putting them together truly makes them sensational.

Yield: 16 BLTs, about 1 heaping cup (320 g) guacamole

For the guacamole:

2 small ripe avocados, halved, pitted, and peeled

2 tablespoons (8 g) soft sun-dried tomato halves (not oil-packed), minced (optional)

1½ tablespoons (15 g) minced red onion

½ teaspoon (up to 1 teaspoon) minced jalapeño pepper, to taste (optional)

1½ tablespoons (2 g) chopped fresh cilantro or fresh parsley (optional)

1 to 1½ tablespoons (15 to 23 ml) fresh lime or lemon juice

Smoked Paprika Salt (page 24) or fine sea salt, to taste

For the bacon and BLTs:

1 recipe Shiitake Bacon (page 39), made with 2 large portobello mushrooms (about 7 ounces, or 198 g total)

16 slices (½-inch, or 1.3 cm, thick) baguette, toasted

4 romaine leaves, torn into pieces

1 large tomato, sliced into ¼-inch (6 mm) rounds and cut in half to make 16 slices

To make the guacamole: Mash the avocado with the sun-dried tomatoes, onion, jalapeño, cilantro, lime juice, and salt to taste. You can leave the guacamole slightly chunky if you prefer. Store in an airtight container in the refrigerator. Use promptly after preparation.

To make the bacon: Use portobellos, stems and gills removed, instead of shiitake mushrooms. The marinade is the same, but increase the heat to 400°F (200°C, or gas mark 6), and bake the mushrooms on 2 parchment-lined rimmed baking sheets in a single layer. Bake for 20 to 25 minutes, until quite dark. The mushrooms should look dry and reduce by about two-thirds. If overbaked, they will be bitter. If underbaked, return to the oven in 3-minute increments. The bacon will crisp as it cools.

To assemble the BLTs, spread the guacamole evenly on the toasted baguette slices. Divide the lettuce leaves evenly on the toast, and top each with a tomato and a few slices of portobello bacon. Serve promptly to prevent the guacamole from discoloring.

> **RECIPE NOTE**
>
> There is no need to increase the baking liquid from the shiitake bacon to make the portobello bacon, due to different moisture levels in the mushrooms.

FIG AND NUT CANAPÉS

We've made many nut spreads in the past, but this one might be the best! We love the mousse-like texture, creaminess, and whiteness the coconut cream imparts to this spread. These canapés (a fancy way to say bread or crackers with topping) are also excellent without the fig spread, if you're not in a figgy mood.

Yield: 32 canapés, about 2 cups (544 g) cashew almond spread

For the cashew almond spread:

1½ cups (210 g) raw cashews

½ cup (56 g) slivered almonds

¼ cup plus 2 tablespoons (90 ml) water, extra 2 tablespoons (30 ml) if needed

1 tablespoon plus 1 teaspoon (20 ml) fresh lemon juice

¼ cup (50 g) coconut cream, scooped from the top of a chilled can of full-fat coconut milk (see Glossary, page 11)

½ teaspoon fine sea salt

For the canapés:

1⅓ cups (389 g, about 2 recipes) Fig Spread (page 146)

1 sourdough (16-inch, or 41 cm, long), baguette, cut into ½-inch (1.3 cm) slices, lightly toasted

2 cups (544 g) Cashew Almond Spread

2 ripe, firm pears, each sliced into 32 thin wedges

Brown rice syrup, for drizzling

¾ cup (90 g) chopped toasted walnuts

To make the cashew almond spread: Place the cashews and almonds in a 4-cup (940 ml) glass measuring cup. Generously cover with water. Cover with plastic wrap, and let stand at room temperature for 8 hours to soften the nuts.

Drain the nuts (discard the soaking water); give them a quick rinse. Place them in a food processor or high-speed blender, along with the ¼ cup plus 2 tablespoons (90 ml) water, lemon juice, coconut cream, and salt. Process until perfectly smooth, stopping to scrape the sides occasionally with a rubber spatula. If you see that the nuts need extra moisture to blend easily, add up to 2 extra tablespoons (30 ml) water, 1 tablespoon (15 ml) at a time. This might take up to 10 minutes, depending on the machine.

Transfer the spread into a medium-size bowl fitted with a lid, and let stand at room temperature for 24 hours. After 24 hours, the top of the spread will look slightly crackled, and the spread will be mousse-like; store in an airtight container in the refrigerator for up to 2 weeks.

To make the canapés: Spread 2 teaspoons of fig spread on each slice of bread, or enough to thinly cover the surface of the bread. Add 1 tablespoon (17 g) cashew almond spread on top, or enough to generously cover the surface of the bread. Add two pear wedges per slice. Lightly drizzle with the syrup, using a fork or a honey dipper. Drop a few chopped walnuts on top. Serve immediately.

EGGPLANT STACKERS

Think eggplant Parmesan, boosted with pesto, topped with tomato, and made vegan. And *voilà*: You get this mouthwatering stacker.

Yield: 16 stackers

For the bread:

2 tablespoons (30 ml) olive oil

1 teaspoon nutritional yeast

Pinch Italian herb blend

Pinch fine sea salt

Pinch ground black pepper

16 slices (½-inch, or 1.3 cm, thick) French bread

For the eggplant:

¾ cup (60 g) panko crumbs

½ teaspoon Italian herb blend

Salt and pepper, to taste

3 tablespoons (45 ml) unsweetened plain vegan milk

1 tablespoon (8 g) cornstarch

½ teaspoon garlic powder

Nonstick cooking spray

16 slices (½-inch, or 1.3 cm, thick) eggplant

For the pesto:

¾ cup (18 g) fresh basil leaves, plus 16 leaves for garnish

1 or 2 cloves garlic, pressed, to taste

2 tablespoons (18 g) toasted pine nuts or (15 g) toasted walnut pieces

Salt and pepper, to taste

1 tablespoon (15 ml) fresh lemon juice

2 tablespoons to ¼ cup (30 to 60 ml) extra-virgin olive oil, as needed

16 tomato slices (¼-inch, or 6 mm, thick)

To make the bread: Preheat the oven to 400°F (200°C, or gas mark 6). Stir together the oil, nutritional yeast, and seasonings in a small bowl. Brush on one side of each bread slice. Place on a baking sheet, and bake for 10 minutes. These can be made in advance, cooled, and stored in an airtight container for up to 2 days.

To make the eggplant: If you have prepared the bread ahead of time, preheat the oven to 400°F (200°C, or gas mark 6) again. Combine the panko, herb blend, and a generous pinch of salt and pepper on a plate. Whisk together the milk, cornstarch, garlic powder, and a generous pinch of salt and pepper in a shallow dish. Lightly coat a baking sheet with cooking spray. Dip the eggplant slices into the milk mixture, then dredge in the crumb mixture, patting to coat. Put the slices on the baking sheet, and bake for 25 minutes. Turn over and bake for 10 minutes longer, until golden.

To make the pesto: Place the ¾ cup (18 g) basil, garlic, and nuts in a food processor. Pulse a few times to chop the basil and nuts. Add salt and pepper to taste, then add the lemon juice. Slowly add the oil through the hole in the lid while the machine is running, until a paste forms. Leftover pesto can be stored covered in the refrigerator for up to 4 days.

To assemble, spread a layer of pesto on each slice of bread, dividing it evenly among the slices. Top with a tomato slice and a slice of eggplant. Top with a basil leaf. Serve immediately.

RECIPE NOTE

If the eggplant or tomato are larger in diameter than the bread, cut them in half when assembling.

SWEET-AND-SOUR SLOPPY JOES

We can read minds and know what you're thinking: Open-faced Sloppy Joes couldn't possibly be served as finger food now, could they? Especially not with company around. Our testers were skeptical at first too, but let us reassure you that they all enjoyed a mess-less meal, leaving us to ponder whether we should rename these Not-So-Sloppy Joes . . .

Yield: 8 open-faced sandwiches

1 tablespoon (15 ml) neutral-flavored oil

8 ounces (227 g) tempeh, steamed and crumbled

¼ cup plus 2 tablespoons (56 g) minced green bell pepper

¼ cup (40 g) minced red onion

2 tablespoons (31 g) minced pineapple, plus extra for garnish

1 teaspoon ground cumin

2 cloves garlic, minced

1½ teaspoons minced fresh thyme, plus extra for garnish

½ cup (132 g) organic ketchup

2 tablespoons (28 g) packed light brown sugar

1 to 2 tablespoons (15 to 30 ml) red wine vinegar, to taste

2 tablespoons (30 ml) tamari

1 teaspoon vegan Worcestershire sauce

1 teaspoon Dijon mustard

½ teaspoon liquid smoke (optional)

Salt and pepper, to taste

4 vegan English muffins, split and toasted

Heat the oil in a large skillet over medium-high heat. Add the tempeh and cook until lightly browned, stirring occasionally, about 5 minutes. Add the bell pepper, onion, pineapple, cumin, garlic, and thyme. Cook and stir for 1 minute longer.

Add the ketchup, brown sugar, vinegar, tamari, Worcestershire sauce, mustard, and liquid smoke. Reduce the heat to low, and simmer for 10 minutes, stirring occasionally. The sauce will thicken. Taste and adjust the seasonings. Salt and pepper to taste.

Spoon ¼ cup (65 g) onto each English muffin half and garnish with a few pieces of pineapple and a sprinkle of thyme. Serve immediately.

SERVING SUGGESTIONS & VARIATIONS

Make these with black-eyed peas instead! Replace the tempeh with 1 can (15 ounces, or 425 g) black-eyed peas, drained and rinsed. Heat 2 teaspoons of oil in a large skillet over medium-high heat. Add the bell pepper, onion, pineapple, cumin, garlic, and thyme. Cook for 1 minute.

Add the beans, ketchup, brown sugar, vinegar, tamari, Worcestershire sauce, mustard, and liquid smoke. Reduce the heat to low and simmer for 10 minutes, stirring occasionally. Partially crush the beans with a potato masher as you cook them: You don't want them to turn into a paste, but crushing them will allow the sauce to thicken, and also make it easier to eat because whole beans might roll off the bread.

Taste and adjust the seasonings. Spoon ¼ cup (75 g) onto each English muffin half and garnish with a few pieces of pineapple and a sprinkle of thyme.

MUHAMMARA PIT-ZA WEDGES

Get ready to be blown away by the flavor of these pit-za wedges that closely resembles that of non-vegan pizza, even though they're not made from actual marinara and cheese. The muhammara is also outstanding served as a dip with pita chips. If you want to make your wedges even fancier, serve them with bowls of chopped raw veggies to add on top, such as red onion and green bell pepper slices, pitted black olives, and lightly steamed tiny cauliflower florets.

Yield: 40 pita quarters, 1¼ cups (335 g) muhammara

⅓ cup (27 g) panko crumbs

⅓ cup (40 g) walnut pieces

1 jar (12 ounces, or 355 ml) fire-roasted red bell pepper, thoroughly drained

1 or 2 cloves garlic, pressed, to taste

¼ teaspoon ground cumin

2 tablespoons (32 g) tahini

2 tablespoons (30 ml) extra-virgin or regular olive oil

2 teaspoons fresh lemon juice

¼ teaspoon Smoked Paprika Salt (page 24) or fine sea salt, to taste

⅛ teaspoon cayenne pepper

1¼ cups (335 g) Cashew Almond Spread (page 121)

10 pita breads (8-inch, or 20 cm, round)

Combine the panko, walnuts, bell pepper, garlic, cumin, tahini, oil, lemon juice, salt, and cayenne pepper in a food processor. Process until combined but only relatively smooth, stopping to scrape down the sides once with a rubber spatula. Store the muhammara in an airtight container in the refrigerator for at least 2 hours or up to 2 days before serving, to let the flavors meld and the mixture thicken slightly. Stir before serving.

Preheat the oven to 375°F (190°C, or gas mark 5). Have two large baking sheets handy.

To assemble, spread 2 tablespoons (33 g) cashew almond spread on each pita bread. Top with 2 tablespoons (33 g) muhammara, spreading it evenly across the bread. Depending on the size of your baking sheet, you should be able to fit four or five pita breads per sheet. Bake for 15 minutes, until golden brown and crispy. Cut each pita bread into quarters, and serve warm.

SUGGESTIONS AND VARIATIONS

If you can find mini vegan pita breads, that's even better for individual pit-zas that don't need to be cut. Spread 1½ to 2 teaspoons of each spread on top, and bake at the same temperature for 8 to 10 minutes, or until crispy. You will get 30 mini pit-zas if you use 2 teaspoons of spread per mini pita.

RECIPE NOTE

Remember that the Cashew Almond Spread needs to be prepared 2 days in advance!

Sweet Little Somethings

Satisfy your sweet tooth with a few fun and delicious little treats to round out the perfect finger food meal.

Now wait a minute, the party's not over yet! So don't leave the buffet table too soon. Stick around for joy in the shape of fancied-up fruit, must-have candies, smashing cookies, and wee little cakes.

GINGER-MANGO ICE LOLLIES

We recommend serving these sorbet-like, exotic-flavored lollies with our Creamsicle Ice Lollies (page 130, see photo at right) for a satisfying pop of color and flavor contrast.

Yield: 3 cups (705 ml) mixture, 12 small lollies

½ cup (120 ml) water

¼ cup (48 g) evaporated cane juice (see Glossary, page 11)

¼ cup (48 g) Sucanat

3 to 4 tablespoons (18 to 24 g) peeled, sliced fresh ginger, or 1 to 1½ teaspoons ground ginger, to taste

1 pound (454 g) fresh or frozen mango chunks (thawed if frozen)

½ cup (120 ml) fresh orange juice

12 wooden ice lolly sticks

Bring the water, evaporated cane juice, and Sucanat to a boil in a medium-size, heavy-bottomed saucepan over medium-high heat. Lower the heat, and cook until the sugar crystals are dissolved, about 2 minutes, stirring occasionally. Add the ginger slices.

Remove from the heat. Steep the mixture for at least 30 minutes. Pour the syrup through a fine-mesh sieve, directly into a blender. Discard the ginger slices. (If using ground ginger instead of fresh, add it alongside the sugars and water to boil; there's no steeping time needed.) Let cool.

Add the mango chunks and orange juice to the blender, and blend until perfectly smooth.

Pour a scant ¼ cup (60 ml) of the mixture into twelve 2¼-ounce (67 ml) shot glasses, leaving a little under ¼-inch (6 mm) space from the top to allow for expansion as the mixture freezes. Freeze for approximately 2 hours, or until the preparation is solid enough to hold the lolly stick upright. Insert the sticks in the center of all lollies. Freeze overnight. To release the lollies from their molds easily, run tepid water on the outside of the molds for a few seconds. Serve immediately, or place back in the freezer until ready to serve. Store leftovers in an airtight container in the freezer for up to 2 weeks.

SERVING SUGGESTIONS & VARIATIONS

Not a fan of mango? Replace it with 1 pound (454 g) fresh or frozen pineapple chunks (thawed if frozen) instead. Or try this blend: Use 8 ounces (227 g) fresh or frozen mango chunks combined with 8 ounces (227 g) fresh or frozen pineapple chunks, for a tropical-flavored duo of charm.

CREAMSICLE ICE LOLLIES

A super creamy, summery treat *par excellence*, these are to-die-for when served alongside our Ginger-Mango Ice Lollies (page 128) to offer a flavor variety to your guests and satisfy everyone. Be sure to serve them straight from the freezer, as these lollies will melt in the blink of an eye in the summer heat!

Yield: 4 cups (940 ml) mixture, 16 small lollies

For the lemonade concentrate:

¼ cup (48 g) evaporated cane juice (see Glossary, page 11)

¼ cup (60 ml) fresh blood orange juice or regular orange juice

¼ cup (60 ml) fresh lemon juice

For the lollies:

1½ cups (360 g) plain or vanilla vegan yogurt

1½ cups (355 ml) full-fat canned coconut milk

¼ cup plus 2 tablespoons (90 ml) light agave nectar

Zest of 1 organic orange (optional)

16 wooden ice lolly sticks

To make the lemonade concentrate: Combine all the ingredients in a small, heavy-bottomed saucepan. Bring to a boil, lower the heat, and cook until the sugar crystals are dissolved, about 2 minutes, stirring occasionally. Remove from the heat and let cool completely before using.

To make the lollies: Blend together the lemonade concentrate, yogurt, coconut milk, agave nectar, and zest in a blender until perfectly smooth and combined. Pour a scant ¼ cup (60 ml) of the mixture into sixteen 2¼-ounce (67 ml) shot glasses, leaving a little under ¼ inch (6 mm) space from the top to allow for expansion as the mixture freezes.

Freeze for approximately 2 hours, or until the preparation is solid enough to hold the lolly stick upright. Insert sticks in the center of all ice lollies. Freeze overnight. To release the lollies from their molds easily, run tepid water on the outside of the molds just for a few seconds. Enjoy these as soon as they are out of their molds, or return them to the freezer until the very moment you are ready to serve them: They do melt easily. Store leftovers in an airtight container in the freezer for up to 2 weeks.

RECIPE NOTE

For tarter lollies, cut the amount of agave in half, using a total of 3 tablespoons (45 ml) instead. Dip a finger in the mixture to have a taste and see whether you want to add a little more agave.

SERVING SUGGESTIONS & VARIATIONS

If you want to use the lemonade concentrate to make actual lemonade, you can prepare a larger batch of it from the get-go, always using the same ratio of sugar, orange juice, and lemon juice, and combine 1 part lemonade concentrate with 3 to 4 parts chilled water, sparkling water, or unsweetened tea, to taste.

SWEET NACHOS

If your sweet tooth is so almighty that in your world, even nachos have to be sweet, then hold on to your party hats because we've got the party snack of your party dreams right here.

Yield: 4 to 6 servings, ⅔ cup (160 g) nut butter sauce

2 tablespoons (32 g) tahini or other nut butter, slightly heated

¼ cup (64 g) natural almond butter or other nut butter, slightly heated

2 tablespoons (30 ml) brown rice syrup, pure maple syrup, or light agave nectar, slightly heated, more if needed

¼ teaspoon pure vanilla extract

⅛ teaspoon ground cinnamon

2 tablespoons (30 ml) any plain or vanilla vegan milk, as needed

1 Granny Smith apple, quartered, cored, and thinly sliced

1 Pink Lady or any red-skinned apple, quartered, cored, and thinly sliced

1 ripe but firm Bosc or any pear, quartered, cored, and thinly sliced

1 tablespoon (15 ml) fresh lemon juice

2 tablespoons (18 g) cacao nibs or (22 g) coarsely chopped vegan chocolate

¼ cup (45 g) pomegranate seeds

¼ cup (28 g) slivered almonds, toasted

¼ cup (20 g) shredded coconut, toasted

In a medium-size bowl, combine the tahini, almond butter, brown rice syrup, vanilla extract, and cinnamon. Add milk as needed to obtain a pourable but not too thin caramel-like sauce. Adjust the amount of sweetener to taste. Set aside.

Place the apple and pear slices in a large bowl. Add the lemon juice and stir to coat so that the slices don't brown. Shake to remove excess juice.

Place the apple and pear slices on a large serving plate. Pour the sauce on top, and sprinkle evenly with the cacao nibs, pomegranate seeds, slivered almonds, and shredded coconut. Serve immediately.

SUGGESTIONS AND VARIATIONS

For an individual eating experience, make these into four smaller plates rather than one large plate: Simply use a quarter of both apples and a quarter of the pear per plate, and divide the rest of the ingredients accordingly on each smaller plate.

RECIPE NOTES

- To toast shredded coconut and almonds, place them on a rimmed baking sheet. Preheat the oven to 300°F (150°C or gas mark 2). Bake the coconut and almonds until light golden brown, about 8 minutes, checking and stirring every 2 minutes, to make sure they don't burn. Remove from the oven and set aside until serving.

- If you have trouble finding pomegranate seeds, try this instead: Rehydrate ¼ cup (40 g) dried cranberries or dried cherries in 2 tablespoons (30 ml) heated cranberry, cherry, or pomegranate juice for about 1 hour, stirring halfway through, draining before use.

CARAMELIZED BANANAS WITH CHOCOLATE CHIPOTLE SAUCE

In a matter of minutes, you can serve this elegant sweet snack. If you're not a fan of bananas, use pineapple chunks instead. We like using the pretzel sticks here because of the added bonus of dipping them directly into the chocolate, but toothpicks can also be used. If your strawberries are small, you can leave them whole.

Yield: 12 to 14 skewers

- 2 tablespoons (28 g) vegan butter
- ¼ cup (56 g) packed brown sugar
- 2 teaspoons pure maple syrup
- Pinch ground nutmeg
- Pinch fine sea salt
- 2 bananas, cut into 1-inch (2.5 cm) pieces (12 to 14 slices total)
- 1 tablespoon (11 g) vegan semisweet chocolate chips
- 1 tablespoon (15 ml) vegan milk
- 1 teaspoon pure vanilla extract
- Pinch chipotle chile powder
- 12 to 14 thin pretzel sticks or toothpicks
- 6 or 7 strawberries, stems removed, sliced in half lengthwise (see headnote)

Melt the butter in a small skillet over medium heat. Add the sugar, maple syrup, nutmeg, and salt. Cook, stirring, until the mixture is bubbly and the sugar has dissolved, 2 to 3 minutes. Add the bananas, and cook, stirring gently to avoid breaking the bananas, for about 2 minutes. The bananas should remain somewhat firm. With a slotted spoon, remove the bananas to a plate and set aside.

Remove the skillet from the heat, and add the chocolate chips, milk, vanilla, and chile powder. Stir continuously until the chocolate chips are melted. Pour into a shallow serving bowl. Using pretzel sticks or toothpicks, skewer a strawberry half, then a banana slice. Continue until all the fruit is used. Serve immediately.

DOUBLE DECADENCE CHOCOLATE BERRIES

These are a sight for sore eyes, and for hungry party mouths! It's hard to give an exact yield here, as strawberries vary in size. Be sure to have a little extra of everything handy just in case you need to adapt to the size of your berries.

Yield: 14 strawberries, 1½ cups (310 g) filling

For the cream filling:

½ cup plus ⅓ cup (146 g) vegan semisweet chocolate chips, divided

½ cup (130 g) Cashew Almond Spread (page 121)

¼ cup plus 2 tablespoons (75 g) coconut cream, scooped from the top of a chilled can of full-fat coconut milk (see Glossary, page 11)

¼ cup (30 g) vanilla-flavored powdered sugar (see Recipe Note, page 143) or regular powdered sugar

½ teaspoon pure almond extract

For the berries:

1 teaspoon melted coconut oil

1 pound (454 g) large fresh strawberries (about 14), washed, patted dry, hulled, and hollowed

¾ cup (90 g) dry-roasted peanuts or other favorite nut, finely chopped

To make the cream filling: Place ½ cup (88 g) of the chocolate chips in a double boiler and melt over medium heat, stirring until smooth. If you don't have a double boiler, simply place a metal mixing bowl over a pot of simmering water. Be careful not to get any of the water in the chocolate, or it will seize.

Place the spread, coconut cream, powdered sugar, almond extract, and melted chocolate in a food processor. Process until perfectly smooth and combined, stopping to scrape the sides with a rubber spatula. Transfer to a medium-size bowl, cover with a lid or plastic wrap, and refrigerate to thoroughly firm up, about 4 hours.

To make the berries: Place the remaining ⅓ cup (58 g) chocolate chips and the oil in a double boiler and melt over medium heat, stirring until smooth. (See above if you don't have a double boiler.)

Dip each thoroughly dried strawberry in the melted chocolate, almost all the way to the top, or as much as will allow you to hold the berry with your fingers without it being messy. Let the excess chocolate drip back into the bowl. Roll each strawberry in the chopped nuts. Place the dipped berries on a piece of wax paper to let the chocolate set for about 1 hour.

Put the chilled cream filling into a pastry bag fitted with a large decorative tip. Generously fill each strawberry. Serve shortly thereafter, as the strawberries themselves taste best when they are not refrigerated.

GLUTEN-FREE
POTENTIAL

TAHINI CARAMEL POPCORN

Popcorn being one of the most quintessential finger foods there is, we had no choice but to include a recipe for it here. We love the extra nutty flavor the tahini adds to the caramel, making these reminiscent of those crunchy, sweet sesame treats that are unfortunately often prepared with honey.

Yield: 12 ounces (340 g)

For the popcorn:

1½ tablespoons (23 ml) grapeseed or peanut oil

¼ cup (46 g) unpopped popcorn kernels

Pinch fine sea salt

For the caramel:

1 cup (200 g) light brown sugar (not packed)

¼ cup (60 ml) brown rice syrup

2 tablespoons (30 ml) water

Pinch fine sea salt

¼ cup (64 g) tahini

1 teaspoon pure vanilla extract

¼ teaspoon baking soda

RECIPE NOTES

- If you happen to have good-quality, al-ready-popped popcorn handy, you will need 5 cups (70 g) of it for this recipe.

- The dishes will look like a sticky mess, but all you need to do is soak them in hot water for a little bit, and you won't have to scrub hard.

To pop the corn: Heat the oil in a large skillet over medium-high heat. Add a few kernels to the oil, cover the skillet with a lid, and wait to hear the kernels pop. As soon as they pop, you can add the remaining kernels to the skillet, cover it with a lid again, and remove it from the heat for 30 seconds. Return the skillet to the heat. The kernels should start popping all at the same time. Shake the skillet to prevent the popped corn from burning. Lift the lid to release steam, and try to keep it lifted. Once the popping slows down a lot, remove the skillet from the burner. You will need 5 cups (70 g) of popped corn for this recipe, which is what the yield should be, but measure it for the sake of accuracy. Place the popped corn in a large bowl. Add a pinch of salt, and shake to combine. Set aside, and have a silicone baking mat or a large piece of parchment paper handy.

To make the caramel: Combine the sugar, syrup, water, and salt in a heavy-bottomed medium-size pot and cook over medium heat until the sugar is dissolved, about 2 minutes. Bring the mixture to a low boil, reduce the heat to medium-low, and cook for 8 minutes, stirring occasionally. Remove from the heat, and stir the tahini into the mixture until smooth. Add the vanilla and baking soda, stirring to combine. Immediately pour the hot mixture on top of the popcorn, and stir quickly to coat. Place the popcorn on the baking mat or parchment paper to cool completely before breaking apart. Store in an airtight container. Serve within 2 days of preparation.

CINNAMON-GLAZED NUTS

Perfectly spiced and not overly sweet, these walnuts are quick and easy and get rave reviews. You might want to have copies of this recipe on hand—one taste and your guests will be asking for it!

Yield: 2 cups (255 g) glazed nuts

Nonstick cooking spray

3 tablespoons (45 ml) pure maple syrup

2 tablespoons (28 g) packed brown sugar

1 tablespoon (15 ml) neutral-flavored oil

¾ teaspoon ground cinnamon

½ teaspoon pure vanilla extract

Generous pinch ground allspice

Pinch fine sea salt

2 cups (227 g) walnut or pecan halves, or a mix of the two

Preheat the oven to 325°F (170°C, or gas mark 3). Line a large rimmed baking sheet with parchment paper. Lightly coat the paper with cooking spray.

Stir together the maple syrup, sugar, oil, cinnamon, vanilla, allspice, and salt in a medium-size bowl. Add the nuts, and stir to coat. Spread the nuts on the baking sheet in a single layer. Bake for 15 to 17 minutes. The glaze will be bubbly on the nuts. Let cool on the baking sheet, stirring occasionally to coat the nuts with any glaze remaining on the parchment paper. Cool completely, break apart, and store in an airtight container at room temperature.

BETTER BUCKEYES

Buckeyes are a tradition in Ohio, but we opted to update them. We reduced the amount of sugar, so ours aren't cloyingly sweet, and added puffed rice cereal for a surprising crunch! While we were at it, we added a bit of cinnamon, too, because peanut butter loves cinnamon. And so do we.

Yield: 12 buckeyes

2 tablespoons (28 g) vegan butter

½ cup (128 g) no-stir creamy peanut butter

1 teaspoon pure vanilla extract

½ cup (60 g) powdered sugar, sifted

½ teaspoon ground cinnamon

1 tablespoon (15 ml) vegan milk, if needed

¾ cup (23 g) natural puffed rice cereal

¾ cup (132 g) vegan semisweet chocolate chips

Kosher sea salt, to garnish

Line a rimmed baking sheet with wax paper or a silicone baking mat.

Using a hand mixer, cream the butter, peanut butter, and vanilla in a medium-size bowl. Mix in the powdered sugar and cinnamon. The mixture may be slightly crumbly. Add up to 1 tablespoon (15 ml) milk, if needed, to make an easy-to-form dough that is the consistency of very thick frosting. Using your hands, mix in the cereal.

Put the mixture into the freezer for 15 minutes (up to 45 minutes), until the mixture is firm enough to shape easily. Roll into 12 balls, using 1 tablespoon (20 g) of dough per ball. Place the balls on the baking sheet, and refrigerate while melting the chocolate chips; they can also be frozen for 30 minutes to help them firm up, if necessary.

Using a double boiler, melt the chocolate chips over simmering water, stirring constantly.

Remove the buckeye balls from the refrigerator. Stick a toothpick into a buckeye ball, and dip into the chocolate mixture to nearly cover, but still leaving a bit of the dough exposed to look like a buckeye. Return to the baking sheet, and repeat with the remaining balls. Sprinkle each with a pinch of salt. Refrigerate for 30 minutes, or until the chocolate is set. Store in the refrigerator in an airtight container for up to 1 week.

RECIPE NOTES

• It's important to use no-stir peanut butter here (brands vary), or you'll need to dramatically increase the sugar to get the right texture.

• If you don't have a double boiler, see the alternative method in the Nutty Caramel Chocolate Bites (page 141).

MAKE
AHEAD

VANILLA CREAM TARTLETS

It's been proven many times before: No one can say no to an individually sized, portable tartlet! Especially not when the tartlets in question are turned into the life of the party dessert tray when decorated with beautiful fresh berries and dusted with extra vanilla-flavored sugar.

Yield: 12 tartlets

For the filling:

½ cup (60 g) vanilla-flavored powdered sugar (see Recipe Note), plus extra for garnishing

1⅓ cups (192 g) Whipped Coconut Cream (page 163)

½ cup plus 2 tablespoons (163 g) Cashew Almond Spread (page 121)

Zest from ½ organic lemon

For the crusts and garnish:

Nonstick cooking spray

1¾ cups (210 g) whole wheat pastry flour

¼ teaspoon fine sea salt

¼ cup (60 ml) neutral-flavored oil

¼ cup (60 ml) pure maple syrup

2 tablespoons (30 ml) cold water, as needed

1 package (6 ounces, or 170 g) fresh raspberries, rinsed and patted dry

1 package (4.4 ounces, or 125 g) fresh blueberries, rinsed, patted dry

RECIPE NOTE

To make vanilla-flavored powdered sugar, combine 1 cup (120 g) powdered sugar with a split vanilla bean in an airtight container for 2 days. There will be ⅓ cup (40 g) left over after use in this recipe, and it can be used anywhere powdered sugar is called for.

To make the filling: Remove the vanilla bean from the sugar. Place the cream, spread, sugar, and zest in a large bowl. Scrape the seeds from the vanilla bean on top. Gently fold to combine so as not to remove the fluff from the whipped cream. Cover with plastic wrap, and store in the refrigerator for 2 hours or overnight to firm up.

To make the crusts: Preheat the oven to 350°F (180°C, or gas mark 4). Lightly coat twelve 3-inch (7.5 cm) tart pans with cooking spray.

Stir the flour and salt together in a medium-size bowl. Drizzle in the oil and syrup, stirring with a fork to create crumbs. Add the water 1 tablespoon (15 ml) at a time if needed, stirring until a dough forms. Gather the dough on a piece of parchment paper or silicone baking mat. Divide the dough into twelve equal portions, each about 1 ounce (30 g).

Pat each portion down into a 2½-inch (6 cm) circle. Place the circle into the prepared tart pan, and press down on the bottom and just halfway up the edges, about ½ inch (1.3 cm). Repeat with the remaining dough. Prick the crust bottoms with a fork.

Bake for 13 minutes, or until the crusts are light golden brown. Let cool completely in the pans, then remove from the pans before assembling.

Add 2 tablespoons (35 g) of filling per cooled crust.

Place back into the refrigerator for 2 hours to set. Decorate with berries before serving. Sift powdered sugar on top, if desired. These are best served freshly made.

PB&J TARTLETS

We're already placing bets that you will be smitten with the tender crust of these tartlets and their creamy richness made sweetly brighter thanks to the addition of your favorite flavor of jam or jelly. Personally, we're partial to all-fruit, all-natural raspberry jam.

Yield: 12 tartlets

For the crusts:

Nonstick cooking spray

1¾ cups (210 g) whole wheat pastry flour

¼ teaspoon fine sea salt

¼ cup (60 ml) neutral-flavored oil

¼ cup (60 ml) pure maple syrup

2 tablespoons (30 ml) cold water, as needed

For the filling:

¼ cup (80 g) jam or jelly of choice

¾ cup (192 g) natural creamy peanut butter, at room temperature

½ cup (60 g) powdered sugar, more if needed

6 ounces (170 g) vegan semisweet chocolate, finely chopped

To make the crusts: Preheat the oven to 350°F (180°C, or gas mark 4). Lightly coat twelve 3-inch (7.5 cm) quiche or tart pans with cooking spray.

Place the flour, salt, oil, and maple syrup in a food processor. (For instructions on how to make the crust by hand, see Vanilla Cream Tartlets, page 143.) Pulse to combine. Add the water as needed, until a dough forms. Gather the dough on a piece of parchment paper. Divide the dough into twelve equal portions, each about 1 ounce (30 g).

Pat each portion down into an approximately 2½-inch (6 cm) circle. Place the circle into the prepared tart pan, and press it down on the bottom and just halfway up the edges, about ½ inch (1.3 cm). Repeat with the remaining dough. Prick the crust bottoms with a fork.

Bake for 13 minutes, or until the top edges are just slightly golden brown. Let cool completely in the pans, then remove from the pans before assembling.

To make the filling: Place 1 heaping teaspoon of jam in each cooled crust, spreading it evenly. Place in the freezer for 30 minutes to slightly set the jam.

Using an electric mixer, combine the peanut butter with the powdered sugar until a dough forms. Add extra sugar if needed, 1 tablespoon (8 g) at a time, to obtain a firmer dough. Use your hands if needed to make the dough more manageable. Divide into twelve equal portions.

Pat each portion down into an approximately 2-inch (5 cm) circle. Place a circle on top of the firmed-up jam, lightly pressing down to fit the crust.

Melt the chocolate in a double boiler. Place 2 teaspoons of it in the center of each tartlet, spreading it to cover the top. Let the chocolate set before serving, about 30 minutes. Store leftovers in an airtight container at room temperature or in the refrigerator for up to 2 days.

MAKE
AHEAD

CHOCOLATE CHUNK COOKIES

We simply adore the subtle flavor the orange juice gives these perfectly chewy cookies that just beg to be served during a tea party, alongside (what else?) a steaming cup of your favorite tea blend, and a healthy dose of laughter and gossip.

Yield: 24 cookies

¼ cup (60 ml) neutral-flavored oil

¼ cup (55 g) packed light brown sugar

¼ cup plus 2 tablespoons (72 g) evaporated cane juice (see Glossary, page 11)

3 tablespoons plus 1 teaspoon (50 ml) fresh orange juice

1 teaspoon pure vanilla extract

½ teaspoon garam masala or ground cinnamon

½ teaspoon fine sea salt

½ cup (60 g) walnut pieces, chopped

2 ounces (57 g) chopped vegan bittersweet chocolate

1½ cups (180 g) whole wheat pastry flour

½ teaspoon baking powder

Preheat the oven to 350°F (180°C, or gas mark 4). Line two baking sheets with parchment paper or silicone baking mats.

In a large bowl, combine the oil, sugar, evaporated cane juice, orange juice, vanilla, garam masala, salt, walnuts, and chocolate. Sift the flour and baking powder on top of the wet ingredients. Stir to thoroughly combine.

Scoop 1 packed tablespoon (22 g) of dough. You should get approximately twenty-four cookies—twelve cookies per sheet. Leave about 1 inch (2.5 cm) of space between each cookie. Flatten the cookies slightly because they won't spread much while baking.

Bake for 12 minutes: the cookies will look puffy as they come out of the oven, but will collapse slightly after a few minutes. Leave on the sheet for 2 minutes before transferring to a wire rack to cool completely. Once cooled, store leftovers in an airtight container at room temperature for up to 4 days.

RECIPE NOTES

• Not a fan of walnuts? Use the same amount of pecans or almonds in their place.

• If you're skeptical of adding garam masala to your baked goods, you can replace it with the same amount of ground cinnamon. But we urge you to be daring: You'll find that garam masala adds a subtle spicy warmth and richness that rival the awesomeness of the more commonly used cinnamon spice. Pinkie swear.

FIGGY LINZERS

These nutty cookie sandwiches need to be made at least 4 hours before serving to be at their tender best. The filling yields twice the amount needed for this recipe: We use it to make sweet-ish canapés (page 121), as a spread on toast, and alongside vegan cheeses.

Yield: 12 regular linzers, 6 smaller linzers, 1½ cups (438 g) spread

For the fig spread:

8 ounces (227 g) dried figs, stemmed and chopped

Zest of ½ organic orange

1 cup (235 ml) fresh orange juice

2 tablespoons (24 g) Sucanat

Pinch fine sea salt

½ teaspoon pure vanilla extract

For the cookie dough:

3 tablespoons (45 ml) neutral-flavored oil

¼ cup (60 g) plain or vanilla vegan yogurt

¼ cup plus 2 tablespoons (72 g) evaporated cane juice (see Glossary, page 11)

¼ cup plus 2 tablespoons (72 g) Sucanat

1 teaspoon pure vanilla extract

½ teaspoon pure orange extract (optional)

½ cup (60 g) almond meal

1½ cups (180 g) whole wheat pastry flour

1 teaspoon ground cinnamon

½ teaspoon baking powder

½ teaspoon fine sea salt

To make the fig spread: Place the figs, orange zest, orange juice, Sucanat, and salt in a medium-size saucepan. Bring to a boil, lower the heat, and simmer for 15 minutes, stirring occasionally. Remove from the heat, add the vanilla, and stir; cover with a lid, and let cool. Using a blender, blend until mostly smooth. Refrigerate until ready to use.

To make the cookie dough: Preheat the oven to 350°F (180°C, or gas mark 4). Line two baking sheets with parchment paper or silicone baking mats.

Combine the oil, yogurt, evaporated cane juice, Sucanat, and extracts in a medium-size bowl.

Place the almond meal, flour, cinnamon, baking powder, and salt in a food processor. Pulse to combine. Add the wet ingredients, pulsing until a dough forms.

Roll the dough out to a little under ¼-inch (6 mm) thick on a piece of parchment paper. Cut out cookies using a 2½-inch (6 cm) cutter. Place the cookies on the prepared sheets. Repeat with the remaining dough, patting the dough together to roll out again. You should have twenty-four cookies. Use a 1½-inch (4 cm) cutter to remove the center of twelve cookies; the cookie centers need the same baking time.

Bake all the cookies (including the center cut-outs) for 12 minutes, or until the bottoms are light golden brown. Leave on the sheet for 2 minutes before moving to a cooling rack.

Add 1 scant tablespoon (16 g) spread in the center of each whole cookie, without reaching the edges. Place the cookie with the cut-out center on top, and press lightly. Use 1 scant teaspoon of spread (each) on six smaller cookies, and top with another small cookie. Let stand in an airtight container for several hours before serving, to soften. Store leftovers in an airtight container at room temperature for up to 2 days.

THREE-SPICE SNICKERDOODLES

We're not particularly keen on playing favorites, but if you're thinking of building yourself a little cookie buffet for your next sweet-toothed get-together, we wager these funnily named and delicately spiced cookies will be the ones to disappear the quickest.

Yield: 22 cookies

¼ cup plus 1 tablespoon (75 ml) neutral-flavored oil

½ cup plus 1 ½ tablespoons (114 g) evaporated cane juice, divided (see Glossary, page 11)

¼ cup (48 g) light brown sugar (not packed)

2 to 3 tablespoons (30 to 45 ml) plain or vanilla vegan milk, as needed

½ teaspoon pure vanilla extract

Scant 1½ cups (180 g) all-purpose flour

½ teaspoon baking soda

1 teaspoon ground cinnamon, divided

½ teaspoon ground ginger

¼ teaspoon ground nutmeg

½ teaspoon fine sea salt

Preheat the oven to 375°F (190°C, or gas mark 5). Line two baking sheets with parchment paper or silicone baking mats.

Combine the oil, ½ cup (96 g) of the evaporated cane juice, brown sugar, 2 tablespoons (30 ml) of the milk, and vanilla in a large bowl. Combine the flour, baking soda, ½ teaspoon of the cinnamon, ginger, nutmeg, and salt in a medium-size bowl. Stir the dry ingredients into the wet, using your hands if needed. If the dough is too dry and doesn't hold together easily when pinched, add the remaining 1 tablespoon (15 ml) milk, 1 teaspoon at a time.

Use 1 packed tablespoon (20 g) of dough per cookie, placing 11 cookies per sheet with about 1 inch (2.5 cm) of space between each.

Combine the remaining 1½ tablespoons (18 g) evaporated cane juice with the remaining ½ teaspoon cinnamon in a small bowl, and roll each cookie dough ball in the mixture.

Flatten slightly on the prepared sheets, and bake for 8 minutes, until the cookies are puffed. Leave on the baking sheets for 2 minutes before transferring to a wire rack to cool completely. It's important not to leave the cookies on the sheet any longer than that: You want them to firm up, but not dry out. Store leftovers in an airtight container at room temperature for up to 2 days.

ALMOND CRESCENTS

A simple almond-flavored, crescent-shaped shortbread cookie dusted with powdered sugar makes for an especially pleasing treat during the finger food–friendly holiday season. (But these cookies taste so great, and the recipe is so straightforward, that you will probably make them all year long!)

Yield: 17 cookies

½ cup (60 g) almond meal

1¼ cups (150 g) whole wheat pastry flour

3 tablespoons (36 g) evaporated cane juice (see Glossary, page 11)

¼ teaspoon fine sea salt

¼ cup (60 ml) light agave nectar or pure maple syrup

¼ cup (56 g) solid coconut oil, melted

1 teaspoon pure almond extract

½ teaspoon pure vanilla extract

3 tablespoons (23 g) powdered sugar, for dusting

Preheat the oven to 325°F (170°C, or gas mark 3). Line a baking sheet with parchment paper or a silicone baking mat.

Combine the almond meal, flour, sugar, and salt in a food processor. Add the agave nectar, oil, and extracts, pulsing to combine until a dough forms.

Place the dough on the prepared sheet and knead it a couple of times. Using 1 packed tablespoon (20 g) of dough per cookie, form a log, then a small crescent shape, flattening it slightly so that the cookie bakes evenly. You can slightly wet your fingers with water to help make the shaping easier. Leave about 1 inch (2.5 cm) of space between the cookies.

Bake for 18 minutes, or until the cookies are golden brown around the edges and on the bottom. Your nose will tell you when they're just about ready to come out of the oven, so pay close attention.

Carefully transfer the cookies to a wire rack to cool completely. Sift powdered sugar over the cooled cookies. Store leftovers in an airtight container at room temperature for up to 2 days.

SERVING SUGGESTIONS & VARIATIONS

Skip the dusting of powdered sugar and dip half of the cookies (both tips, for example) in melted vegan chocolate instead. We like to keep the chocolate coating to a minimum, that's why we recommend starting with only ¼ cup (44 g) vegan semisweet chocolate chips, and melt more if desired, to avoid leftovers. Place the chocolate chips in a double boiler and melt over medium heat, stirring until smooth. If you don't have a double boiler, simply place a metal mixing bowl over a pot of simmering water. Be careful not to get any of the water in the chocolate, or it will seize.

SWEET PECAN TRIANGLES

We promised you a sweet recipe using the Fry-Anything Dough (page 100), and we're true to our word. These are a little bit like a fried pecan pie, dusted with cinnamon sugar for an extra sweet finish.

Yield: 20 triangles

¼ cup (35 g) raw cashews

1 tablespoon plus 1 teaspoon (20 ml) soy creamer

1 teaspoon pure vanilla extract

½ teaspoon fresh lemon juice

3 tablespoons (23 g) powdered sugar

½ cup (96 g) evaporated cane juice (see Glossary, page 11)

½ teaspoon ground cinnamon

All-purpose flour, for rolling dough

1 recipe Fry-Anything Dough (page 100)

¼ cup plus 3 tablespoons (44 g) minced pecans or walnuts

High-heat neutral-flavored oil, for cooking

Combine the cashews, creamer, vanilla, and lemon juice in a small high-speed blender, and process until completely smooth. Add the powdered sugar. Process until blended.

Lightly flour a baking sheet. Put the evaporated cane juice and cinnamon in a small brown paper bag, and shake to combine.

On a lightly floured surface, roll out half the dough to less than ⅛-inch (3 mm) thick. Cut into twenty 3-inch (7.5 cm) squares, rerolling any scrap dough. Fill each square with ½ teaspoon of the cashew mixture and 1 teaspoon pecans. Fold to form a triangle and carefully seal the edges with wet fingers, patting with flour, if needed. If they are not sealed well, they will leak when frying. Place on the baking sheet, and repeat until all the dough is used.

Line a baking sheet with paper towels for draining. Heat the oil in a deep fryer to 375°F (190°C). Alternatively, heat about 1 inch (2.5 cm) of oil in a heavy-bottomed saucepan. Cook the triangles a few at a time until golden, about 4 minutes. Turn if needed to cook the second side, about 3 minutes. Transfer to the paper towel–lined baking sheet to drain for a minute, then transfer to the sugar and cinnamon bag. Shake to coat. Serve hot, warm, or at room temperature, shortly after making.

SERVING SUGGESTIONS & VARIATIONS

Fill each dough square with 2 teaspoons all-natural raspberry spread. Fry as above. Omit the sugar and cinnamon. Sprinkle with powdered sugar for serving.

GOJI BERRY CACAO BITES

If you prefer keeping your sweet finger food snacks on the more nutritious side of things, we have the super-tempting solution in the form of somewhat chewy little granola bites, filled with add-ins that are open for substitutions, should your preferences differ from ours.

Yield: Approximately 50 bites

2 cups (160 g) old-fashioned oats

½ cup (60 g) toasted wheat germ

½ cup (60 g) almond meal

2 tablespoons (16 g) golden roasted flaxseed

2 tablespoons (30 g) chia seeds

½ cup (60 g) walnut pieces or other chopped nuts

⅓ cup (44 g) dry-roasted sunflower seeds or other seeds/chopped nuts

⅓ cup (45 g) dried goji berries or other dried berries

⅓ cup (47 g) cacao nibs or chopped vegan chocolate

1 teaspoon garam masala or ground cinnamon

½ teaspoon ground ginger

¼ teaspoon fine sea salt

½ cup plus 2 tablespoons (120 g) Sucanat

½ cup (120 ml) light agave nectar

¼ cup (60 ml) neutral-flavored oil

1 teaspoon pure vanilla extract

Line an 8-inch (20 cm) square baking pan with parchment paper.

In a large bowl, combine the oats, wheat germ, almond meal, flaxseed, chia seeds, walnuts, sunflower seeds, goji berries, cacao nibs, garam masala, ginger, and salt.

In a medium-size saucepan, combine the Sucanat, agave, and oil. Bring the mixture to a boil, lower the heat, and simmer for about 2 minutes, until the Sucanat crystals are starting to dissolve. Remove from the heat and stir the vanilla into the wet ingredients. Pour the wet ingredients into the dry, and stir to coat.

Transfer to the prepared baking pan, top with a sheet of wax paper, and press down hard and evenly in the pan. Place the pan in the refrigerator for 2 hours. Invert onto a cutting board and cut into approximately 1¼-inch (3 cm) squares. The preparation might be a little soft still, so just pat it down if anything falls off; it's sticky enough for that.

Preheat the oven to 300°F (150°C, or gas mark 2). Line three baking sheets with parchment paper or silicone baking mats.

Place one-third of the granola bites on each prepared sheet, leaving at least 1 inch (2.5 cm) of space between each.

Bake for 12 to 15 minutes, until just barely golden brown on top. Let cool on the baking sheet for 15 minutes to firm before transferring to a cooling rack. Let cool completely before storing in an airtight container at room temperature for up to 1 week.

MAKE
AHEAD

GRANOLA TRAIL MIX

The huge batch this trail mix recipe yields never lasts very long in our respective households, even when there are no guests around to help us munch on it. Also, stating the obvious: The granola part of the mix is excellent without the extras and paired up with vegan milk for breakfast, turning a rad snack into a spoon-tastic morning cereal.

Yield: 3 pounds (1.4 kg)

¼ cup (60 ml) pure maple syrup

¼ cup (60 ml) brown rice syrup

¼ cup (48 g) Sucanat

1 cup (256 g) unsalted crunchy almond butter or peanut butter

1½ teaspoons pure vanilla extract

¼ cup (60 ml) neutral-flavored oil

Scant ½ teaspoon fine sea salt

2 teaspoons ground cinnamon

½ teaspoon ground ginger

¼ teaspoon allspice

¼ teaspoon ground nutmeg

3 cups (240 g) rolled oats or other rolled flakes (like spelt or rye)

¾ cup (90 g) wheat germ

1 cup (176 g) vegan semisweet chocolate chips

1 cup (147 g) dry-roasted peanuts or coarsely chopped dry-roasted almonds

1 cup (160 g) dried cherries or raisins, or a combination

Preheat the oven to 300°F (150°C or gas mark 2). Have a large rimmed baking sheet handy.

In a large bowl, combine the syrups, Sucanat, nut butter, vanilla, oil, salt, and spices. Stir to emulsify. Add the oats and wheat germ. Stir to thoroughly coat.

Evenly spread the granola on the sheet: The mass of granola is rather cohesive at this stage, so break it into large clusters so that it bakes evenly, rather than leaving it as a huge mass. Bake in 12-minute increments, flipping the granola with a spatula after each increment, being careful not to break the large clusters, for a total of approximately 24 minutes. Continue to bake in shorter (4-minute) increments until the granola is lightly browned and mostly dry: A slight moistness is okay at the end. Let cool on the sheet. The granola will crisp as it cools. Let cool completely before combining with the chocolate chips, peanuts, and cherries.

Store leftovers in an airtight container at room temperature or in the refrigerator for up to 2 weeks.

RECIPE NOTES

- You can replace the almond butter with any nut or seed butter you prefer, and switch the add-ins, too.

- If 3 pounds (1.4 kg) of trail mix sounds like a dangerous thing to have around the house, this recipe is a breeze to halve.

BROWNIE NUT BUTTER CUPS

We've taken a look at the best thing ever (also known as peanut butter cups) and gone one step further, replacing the chocolate candy bottom with a mini brownie. You'll realize what a brilliant idea it was when you get your fingers on (and sink your teeth into) the resulting chewy, super rich goodness!

Yield: 34 mini brownie cups

For the brownies:

Nonstick cooking spray

4 ounces (113 g) vegan chocolate, chopped

3 tablespoons (42 g) solid coconut oil

½ cup (120 g) blended soft silken tofu or plain vegan yogurt

1 cup (200 g) light brown sugar (not packed)

½ teaspoon fine sea salt

2 teaspoons pure vanilla extract

1¼ cups (150 g) whole wheat pastry flour

For the filling:

¾ cup (192 g) creamy natural almond or peanut butter, at room temperature

3 tablespoons (23 g) powdered sugar

Pinch fine sea salt

2 ounces (57 g) vegan chocolate, chopped

To make the brownies: Preheat the oven to 350°F (180°C, or gas mark 4). Lightly coat thirty-four cups of two mini muffin pans with cooking spray.

Place the chocolate and oil in a microwave-safe bowl, and heat in 1-minute increments, until the chocolate is melted and can be easily stirred. (Alternatively, place the chocolate and oil in a small saucepan and slowly warm over low heat until melted.)

In a medium-size bowl, combine the melted chocolate with the tofu, brown sugar, salt, and vanilla. Sift the flour on top, and stir until well combined. Place about 2½ teaspoons brownie batter per cup, filling each cup two-thirds full.

Bake for 12 minutes. The brownies will look a little wet, and will slightly collapse while cooling; this will create the indentation for the filling. If your brownies don't collapse within a few minutes, use the curved back of a ½ teaspoon to indent. Let cool in the pans on a wire rack, then refrigerate for 45 minutes, to easily remove from the pans. In the meantime, prepare the filling.

To make the filling: Combine the nut butter with the powdered sugar and salt in a small bowl. If your nut butter is on the thin side, add a little extra powdered sugar to thicken. Set aside.

Remove the chilled cups from the pans, and place 1 teaspoon filling per indentation. Sprinkle a tiny handful of chocolate on top, pressing down slightly.

Serve chilled. Leftovers may be stored in an airtight container in the refrigerator for up to 1 week.

BLACK FOREST JARS

You caught us red-handed: This dessert is in a jar and needs to be eaten with a spoon. But it's handheld and stores/transports well! Our little fingers tell us you'll forgive us as soon as you dig in . . .

Yield: 6 jars

Nonstick cooking spray

½ cup (120 ml) any vegan milk

½ cup (96 g) evaporated cane juice (see Glossary, page 11)

2 tablespoons (30 ml) neutral-flavored oil

½ teaspoon pure vanilla extract

½ teaspoon pure almond extract, divided

¼ teaspoon fine sea salt

¾ cup (90 g) whole wheat pastry flour

¼ cup (20 g) unsweetened cocoa powder

1 teaspoon baking powder

½ teaspoon cornstarch

2 teaspoons Kirschwasser (optional)

1¼ cups (295 ml) black cherry tea, steeped from 2 teabags, cooled

¼ cup plus 2 tablespoons (120 g) cherry jam or chopped vegan maraschino cherries

1½ cups plus 3 tablespoons (270 g) Whipped Coconut Cream (page 163)

2 tablespoons (17 g) grated vegan chocolate

Preheat the oven to 350°F (180°C, or gas mark 4). Lightly coat eighteen cups of two standard muffin pans with cooking spray.

Combine the milk, sugar, oil, vanilla, ¼ teaspoon of the almond extract, and salt in a large bowl. Sift the flour, cocoa, baking powder, and cornstarch on top. Using an electric mixer, mix until perfectly smooth. Place 1 generous tablespoon (18 g) of batter into each prepared muffin cup.

Bake for 6 to 8 minutes, until the top springs back when touched. Leave the oven on. Carefully remove the cakes from the pan. Let cool for 5 minutes.

Place the cakes on a baking sheet lined with parchment paper, and bake for another 10 minutes; this will prepare the cakes for the tea-soaking. Place on a cooling rack.

Have ready six half-pint (8 ounces, or 235 ml) mason jars with a diameter of more than 2½ inches (6 cm) (or same diameter as your muffin pan holes) so that the cakes fit easily.

Stir the Kirschwasser and remaining ¼ teaspoon almond extract into the tea. Fully soak each cooled cake in the tea for about 10 seconds, only as you assemble the jars, letting the excess liquid drip back into the bowl.

Place a cake at the bottom of a jar. Top with 1½ teaspoons jam. Top with 1½ tablespoons (15 g) whipped cream. Top with another cake. Top with the same quantity of jam and the same quantity of whipped cream. Top with another cake. Top with whipped cream, spreading it evenly. Top with 1 teaspoon grated chocolate. Repeat with the remaining jars. Cover the jars with lids, and refrigerate overnight to let the flavors meld.

Serve chilled, and enjoy within 2 days of preparation. You can also freeze the jars for up to 3 months, thawing them in the refrigerator overnight before serving.

FULL-O-NUTS MINI CUPCAKES

Do you remember the pretty famous (and not vegan) milk chocolate candies that have finely chopped hazelnuts in them? We're told these tender, finger-friendly little cakes are reminiscent of the candies in question. But if you're not a fan of hazelnuts, you can make them with almonds instead. We also find that the longer these sit, the more their flavor develops, so don't be afraid to make the cakes the day before you plan on enjoying them, alone or in good company. Just be sure to add the topping when you're almost ready to serve.

Yield: 42 mini cupcakes

½ cup plus 2 tablespoons (150 g) plain or vanilla vegan yogurt

¾ cup (144 g) evaporated cane juice (see Glossary, page 11)

¼ cup (60 ml) plain or vanilla vegan milk

¼ cup (60 ml) neutral-flavored oil

½ teaspoon fine sea salt

1 teaspoon pure vanilla extract

1 cup (120 g) whole wheat pastry flour

1 cup (120 g) shelled hazelnuts or whole almonds (not skinned)

2 tablespoons (16 g) cornstarch

1½ teaspoons baking powder

½ teaspoon baking soda

½ cup (88 g) chopped vegan chocolate

1 recipe cream filling from Double Decadence Chocolate Berries (page 134)

6 pieces Nutty Caramel Chocolate Bites (page 141), finely chopped (optional)

Preheat the oven to 350°F (180°C, or gas mark 4). Line forty-two cups of two mini muffin pans with paper liners.

In a medium-size bowl, combine the yogurt, sugar, milk, oil, salt, and vanilla.

In a food processor, combine the flour and hazelnuts; process until the hazelnuts are very finely ground. Transfer to a large bowl, and combine with the cornstarch, baking powder, and baking soda. Pour the wet ingredients into the dry and stir just until combined. Gently fold the chopped chocolate into the batter.

Divide the batter among the lined cups, about 2½ teaspoons per liner, filling the liners about two-thirds full. Do not overfill the liners. Bake for 18 to 22 minutes, or until the tops are lightly brown and spring back when touched.

Remove from the muffin pan, and let cool completely on a wire rack. We find these to be at their best several hours after being prepared, or even the next day. Store in an airtight container at room temperature until serving.

Spread or pipe a small amount of cream filling onto each cupcake and add a tiny sprinkle of chopped Nutty Caramel Chocolate Bites on top of each, just before serving.

RECIPE NOTE

If you like a more generous topping, prepare and use 1½ recipes of the cream filling.

MINI RUM RAISIN CUPCAKES

Hopefully, you're not tired of the vegan cupcake revolution yet (imagine us looking at you in disbelief if you actually are), because we just couldn't *not* include a few mini cupcake recipes to make the dessert chapter of this finger food cookbook complete.

Yield: 40 mini cupcakes

For the cupcakes:

½ cup (80 g) raisins

½ cup (120 ml) dark rum

½ cup (120 ml) any vegan milk

¼ cup (60 ml) any neutral-flavored oil

½ cup plus 2 tablespoons (120 g) Sucanat

1½ teaspoons pure vanilla extract

2 cups (240 g) whole wheat pastry flour

1 teaspoon baking powder

1 teaspoon baking soda

1 teaspoon ground nutmeg

½ teaspoon fine sea salt

For the frosting:

6 tablespoons (84 g) vegan butter, softened

6 tablespoons (78 g) vegan shortening

2¼ cups (270 g) powdered sugar

Generous ¼ teaspoon maple extract (or ½ teaspoon pure vanilla extract and ¼ teaspoon ground cinnamon)

⅛ teaspoon fine sea salt

> **RECIPE NOTE**
>
> You can use the same amount of vegan butter if vegan shortening isn't available. The frosting will be softer, so store it in the refrigerator. Decorate the cupcakes when ready to serve.

To make the cupcakes: Combine the raisins and rum in a small saucepan or a microwave-safe bowl. Bring to a boil, and remove from the heat immediately. If using a microwave, heat for 30 seconds and remove from the oven. Let stand for about 10 minutes so the raisins plump up and the preparation cools down again.

Preheat the oven to 325°F (170°C, or gas mark 3). Line forty cups of two mini muffin pans with paper liners.

Combine the rum and raisin preparation, milk, oil, Sucanat, and vanilla in a large bowl.

Sift the flour, baking powder, baking soda, nutmeg, and salt into a medium-size bowl. Add to the wet ingredients, and stir until just combined.

Fill each paper liner about two-thirds full. Bake for 12 to 14 minutes, or until a toothpick inserted into the center comes out clean.

Place the cupcakes on a wire rack to cool completely before frosting.

To make the frosting: Using an electric mixer, cream the butter and shortening. Slowly add the sugar, and beat until combined. Add the maple extract and salt; beat until fluffy, about 2 minutes.

Spread or pipe a small amount of frosting onto each cupcake. Store the (preferably frosting-free) leftovers in an airtight container at room temperature for up to 2 days. Store the frosting leftovers in an airtight container in the refrigerator for up to 2 days. Allow to soften at room temperature to decorate the cupcakes just before serving.

MINI LEMON CUPCAKES

As huge and unabashed chocolate lovers as we may be, we make an exception for any and all lemon-flavored desserts. These tiny bites are reminiscent of lemon meringue pies and will be perfect on a pretty cake stand, flanked by our previous two mini cupcakes recipes, so that those with a sweet tooth can find their flavor match on the dessert table. Better yet, eat one of each!

Yield: 42 mini cupcakes

For the cupcakes:

1 cup (240 g) blended soft silken tofu or vegan yogurt

⅔ cup (127 g) evaporated cane juice (see Glossary, page 11)

⅓ cup (80 ml) neutral-flavored oil

1 teaspoon pure vanilla extract

2 teaspoons pure lemon extract

Zest from 1 organic lemon

1 tablespoon (15 ml) fresh lemon juice

Scant ½ teaspoon fine sea salt

1½ cups (180 g) whole wheat pastry flour

2 teaspoons baking powder

For the frosting:

6 tablespoons (84 g) vegan butter, softened

6 tablespoons (78 g) vegan shortening

2¼ cups (270 g) powdered sugar

Zest from ½ organic lemon or scant ½ teaspoon pure lemon extract

⅛ teaspoon fine sea salt

Few drops natural yellow food coloring (optional)

To make the cupcakes: Preheat the oven to 350°F (180°C, or gas mark 4). Line forty-two cups of two mini muffin pans with paper liners.

In a large bowl, whisk the tofu, evaporated cane juice, oil, extracts, zest, lemon juice, and salt. Add the flour and baking powder on top, and whisk until combined, to eliminate lumps. Divide the batter among the lined cups, about 2½ teaspoons per liner, filling the liners about two-thirds full.

Bake for 20 minutes, or until the tops spring back when touched. Place the cupcakes on a wire rack to cool completely before frosting.

To make the frosting: Using an electric mixer, cream the butter and shortening. Slowly add the sugar and beat until combined. Add the zest or extract and the salt; beat until fluffy, adding just enough drops of food coloring, if desired, for the frosting to obtain the desired color, about 2 minutes.

Spread or pipe a small amount of frosting onto each cupcake. Store the (preferably frosting-free) leftovers in an airtight container at room temperature for up to 2 days. Store the frosting leftovers in an airtight container in the refrigerator for up to 2 days. Allow to soften at room temperature to decorate the cupcakes just before serving.

RECIPE NOTE

You can use the same amount of vegan butter if vegan shortening isn't available or desired: note that the frosting will be softer, so it is preferable to store it in the refrigerator and only decorate the cupcakes when ready to serve.

CHOCOLATE POUND CAKE AND FRUIT SKEWERS

This triple-threat treat looks far more involved than it actually is: make the cream and cake ahead of time, and build the little skewers in a matter of minutes when dessert o'clock rolls around.

Yield: 12 skewers

For the whipped coconut cream:

2 cans (14 ounces, or 414 ml each) full-fat coconut milk (see Glossary, page 11)

½ cup plus 2 tablespoons (75 g) powdered sugar, sifted

For the cake:

Nonstick cooking spray

½ cup (120 g) plain or vanilla vegan yogurt

½ cup (120 ml) any vegan milk

¾ cup (180 ml) light agave nectar

¼ cup (60 ml) melted coconut oil

2 teaspoons pure vanilla extract

1¼ cups plus 2 tablespoons (165 g) whole wheat pastry flour

½ cup (40 g) unsweetened cocoa powder

2 tablespoons (16 g) cornstarch

2 teaspoons baking powder

½ teaspoon fine sea salt

12 skewers (8-inch, or 20 cm, long)

24 small fresh strawberries, rinsed, hulled, and patted dry

24 cubes (1-inch, or 2.5 cm) fresh pineapple

To make the whipped coconut cream: Let the cans settle at room temperature before placing them for at least 24 hours in the refrigerator, along with the bowl used to whip the cream. Scoop the hardened cream from the top of each can, and place it in the chilled bowl along with the sugar. Using an electric mixer with a whisk attachment, whisk until thickened, about 5 minutes. The approximate yield for the whipped cream from two cans is 17 ounces (482 g). Refrigerate in an airtight container until ready to use, up to 2 days before serving.

To make the cake: Preheat the oven to 350°F (180°C, or gas mark 4). Lightly coat an 8 × 4-inch (20 × 10 cm) loaf pan with cooking spray.

Combine the yogurt, milk, agave, oil, and vanilla in a small saucepan over medium heat until barely lukewarm.

Sift the flour, cocoa powder, cornstarch, baking powder, and salt into a large bowl. Add the liquid ingredients, and mix until smooth, using an electric mixer. Pour into the prepared pan.

Bake for 45 minutes, or until a toothpick inserted into the center comes out clean.

Let cool for 15 minutes on a wire rack before removing the cake from the pan. Let the cake cool completely before slicing. Wrap tightly in foil, and store at room temperature for up to 2 days before serving.

Cut the cake into eight 1-inch (2.5 cm) slices. Cut each slice into six cubes. Use four cake cubes per skewer. Skewer a cake cube, a strawberry, another cake cube, pineapple, cake, strawberry, cake, and pineapple at the end. Serve with whipped cream for dipping.

Menu Suggestions

Our humble parting gift to you: a list of menu pairing ideas to inspire you to create beautiful and celebratory spreads for both your guests and yourself. Here's to finger foods for everyone!

American Melting Pot Munchies
Brewpub Cauliflower Dip and Chips, page 17
Sauerkraut-Stuffed Seitan Rounds, page 59
Jamaican Jerk Tempeh Skewers, page 69
Pot Stickers, page 71
X's and O's Focaccia, page 112

An Elegant Evening
"Bacon"-Wrapped Water Chestnuts, page 38
Oven-Steamed Artichokes with Awesome Sauce,
   page 48
Tiny Tomato Pies, page 82
Baked Polenta Fries with Avocado Dip, page 86
Mushroom Toasties, page 113
Fig and Nut Canapés, page 121

Asian Feast
Glazed Sugar Snaps, page 50
Kimchi-Stuffed Sausages, page 60
Pad Thai Summer Rolls, page 88
Sushi Rice Rolls, page 90
Traditional Eggless Rolls, page 93

Breakfast Lovers' Favorites
Baked Frittata Minis, page 72
Hot Pepper Toastwiches, page 114
Sweet Pecan Triangles, page 150

Cinco de Mayo
Rasta Salsa, page 16
Baked Jalapeños, page 36
Baked Lenteja Taquitos, page 77
Mean Bean Taco Cups, page 79
Salsa Scuffins, page 101

Comfort Food Finger Feast
Rainbow Root Veggie Chips, page 24
Potato Puffs with Tapenade, page 43
Brussels Sprouts with Crispy Onions, page 53
Whiz Bangs with Pantry Raid Ranch Dip, page 57
Antipasta Tofu Stuffed Shells, page 85
Portobello BLTs, page 118
Sweet-and-Sour Sloppy Joes, page 125

Extra-Easy Entertaining
Snacking Chickpeas, page 21
Party Olives, page 22
Marinated Mushrooms, page 26
Tree-Hugger Celery Sticks, page 32
Tahini Cauliflower, page 49
Chipotle Almonds, page 58

Game Night, Sports
Year-Round Ratatouille, page 18
Nacho Potato Skins with Nacho Saucy Dip,
   pages 44 and 58
Baked Buffalo Tofu Bites with Pantry
   Raid Ranch, pages 63 and 57
Mini Polenta Rounds, page 64
Moroccan Snack Bars, page 65

Game Night, Board Games
Corn Fritters with Tomato-Thyme Gravy, page 47
Baked Frittata Minis, page 72
Red Pepper Hummus Tartlets, page 80
Sambusas, page 94
Portobello Horseradish Bruschetta, page 117

Hot Summer Night
Harissa Carrot Zucchini Cups, page 30
Mini Bell Pepper Boats, page 33
Kale Cucumber Cups, page 34
Sesame Cucumber Sandwiches, page 40
Ginger-Mango Ice Lollies, page 128
Creamsicle Ice Lollies, page 130

International Happy Hour
Green Beans Jalfrezi, page 49
Banh Mi Lettuce Wraps, page 70
Falafel Fritters with Spicy Tahini Sauce, page 75
Pulled Jackfruit Mini Tacos, page 76
Eggless Roll Smash-Ups, page 92
Muhammara Pit-za Wedges, page 126

Long Walk Lovers' Snack Pack (*Serve with fresh fruit and bottles of cold water.*)
Chipotle Almonds, page 58
Green Snackers, page 99
Goji Berry Cacao Bites, page 151
Granola Trail Mix, page 153

Mediterranean Party Time
Mediterranean Stuffed Mushrooms, page 28
Mediterranean Meatless Balls, page 66
Mini Savory Scones, page 102
Pull-Apart Pesto Bread, page 107
Twisted Bread Sticks, page 108
Spinach Swirls with Quickie Marinara, pages 111 and 16
Eggplant Stackers, page 122

Romance in the Air
Black Lentil Endive Cups, page 29
Potato Towers, page 39
Spears and 'Shrooms, page 54
Creamy Leek Mini Pies, page 81
Lemon-Fennel Scone Bites, page 105
Vanilla Cream Tartlets, page 143

What a Spread!
Smoked Chickpea Hummus, page 20
Red Onion Apple Chutney, page 56
Roasted Eggplant Bread Spread, page 96
Smoky Four-Seed Crackers, page 97
Green Monster Bread, Revisited, page 106

Baby Shower Treats
PB&J Tartlets, page 144
Brownie Nut Butter Cups, page 154
Black Forest Jars, page 157
Full-o-Nuts Mini Cupcakes, page 158
Mini Rum Raisin Cupcakes, page 161
Mini Lemon Cupcakes, page 162

Candy Lovers' Buffet
Tahini Caramel Popcorn, page 135
Cinnamon-Glazed Nuts, page 137
Better Buckeyes, page 138
Chocolate Stout Truffles, page 140
Nutty Caramel Chocolate Bites, page 141

Cookie Bar (*Serve with an assortment of vegan milks in shot glasses.*)
Chocolate Chunk Cookies, page 145
Figgy Linzers, page 146
Three-Spice Snickerdoodles, page 147
Almond Crescents, page 149

Fruit Lovers' Buffet
Sweet Nachos, page 131
Caramelized Bananas with Chocolate Chipotle Sauce, page 133
Double Decadence Chocolate Berries, page 134
Chocolate Pound Cake and Fruit Skewers, page 163

Acknowledgments

Heartfelt thanks to Amanda Waddell, Heather Godin, Betsy Gammons, Karen Levy, Kathy Dragolich, as well as Robert Lesser for their expertise and for turning a simple Word document into a tangible (not to mention, quite pretty) cookbook!

Our better-than-vegan-ice-cream team of testers, whose help made these recipes even more awesomely foolproof: Courtney Blair, Monika Soria Caruso, Kelly and Mac Cavalier, Michelle Cavigliano, Megan Clarke, Shannon Davis, Dorian Farrow, Lisa Miller, Monique and Michel Narbel-Gimzia, Constanze Reichardt, Sara Rose, Stephanie Bly Sulzman, and Vegan Aide.

Celine says, "Thank you, thank you!" to Chaz, Mamou, and Papou. Much gratitude to Tami for being a world-class writing partner and friend.

Tami thanks her family and friends, who were willing tasters, especially Jim, whose feedback is the best (as is his dishwashing), and of course, Celine, for another fun book!

About the Authors

Celine Steen is the coauthor of *500 Vegan Recipes, The Complete Guide to Vegan Food Substitutions, Hearty Vegan Meals for Monster Appetites, Vegan Sandwiches Save the Day!*, and *Whole Grain Vegan Baking*. In addition to developing her own recipes, she has photographed those of other vegan cookbook authors, such as Joni Marie Newman and Natalie Slater. You can find her at www.havecakewilltravel.com and see her portfolio at www.celinesteen.com. Get in touch with her at celine@havecakewilltravel.com.

Tami Noyes is the author of *American Vegan Kitchen* and *Grills Gone Vegan*, and she is the coauthor of *Vegan Sandwiches Save the Day!* and *Whole Grain Vegan Baking*. She lives, cooks, and blogs in her three-kitty home in Ohio. In addition to her blog, www.veganappetite.com, Tami contributes to several vegan sites. E-mail Tami at veganappetite@gmail.com.

Index